3

De

with

Ishmael

NATIONAL DISTRIBUTORS

UK (and countries not listed below): CWR, Waverley Abbey House, Waverley Lane, Farnham, Surrey GU9 8EP. Tel: (01252) 784710 Outside UK (44) 1252 784710

AUSTRALIA: CMC Australasia, PO Box 519, Belmont, Victoria 3216. Tel: (03) 5241 3288

CANADA: CMC Distribution Ltd, PO Box 7000, Niagara on the Lake, Ontario L0S 1J0. Tel: 1800 325 1297

GHANA: Challenge Enterprises of Ghana, PO Box 5723, Accra. Tel: (021) 222437/223249 Fax: (021) 226227

HONG KONG: Cross Communications Ltd, 1/F, 562A Nathan Road, Kowloon. Tel: 2780 1188 Fax: 2770 6229

INDIA: Crystal Communications, 10-3-18/4/1, East Marredpally, Secunderabad – 500 026. Tel/Fax: (040) 7732801

KENYA: Keswick Bookshop, PO Box 10242, Nairobi. Tel: (02) 331692/226047 Fax: (02) 728557

MALAYSIA: Salvation Book Centre (M) Sdn Bhd, 23 Jalan SS 2/64, 47300 Petaling Jaya, Selangor. Tel: (03) 78766411/78766797 Fax: (03) 78757066/78756360

NEW ZEALAND: CMC Australasia, PO Box 36015, Lower Hutt. Tel: 0800 449 408 Fax: 0800 449 049

NIGERIA: FBFM, Helen Baugh House, 96 St Finbarr's College Road, Akoka, Lagos. Tel: (01) 7747429/4700218/825775/827264

PHILIPPINES: OMF Literature Inc, 776 Boni Avenue, Mandaluyong City. Tel: (02) 531 2183 Fax: (02) 531 1960

REPUBLIC OF IRELAND: Scripture Union, 40 Talbot Street, Dublin 1. Tel: (01) 8363764

SINGAPORE: Campus Crusade Asia Ltd, 315 Outram Road, 06-08 Tan Boon Liat Building, Singapore 169074. Tel: 222 3640

SOUTH AFRICA: Struik Christian Books, 80 MacKenzie Street, PO Box 1144, Cape Town 8000. Tel: (021) 462 4360 Fax: (021) 461 3612

SRI LANKA: Christombu Books, 27 Hospital Street, Colombo 1. Tel: (01) 433142/328909

TANZANIA: CLC Christian Book Centre, PO Box 1384, Mkwepu Street, Dar es Salaam. Tel/Fax (022) 2119439

USA: CMC Distribution, PO Box 644, Lewiston, New York, 14092-0644. Tel: 1800 325 1297

ZIMBABWE: Word of Life Books, Shop 4, Memorial Building, 35 S Machel Avenue, Harare. Tel: (04) 781305 Fax: (04) 774739

For e-mail addresses, visit the CWR web site: www.cwr.org.uk

365 Devotions with Ishmael

5 minutes together with God
for every day of the year

Published 2002 by CWR, Waverley Abbey House, Waverley Lane, Farnham, Surrey GU9 8EP.

Design and typesetting: Christine Reissland at CWR Creative Services.

Front cover illustration: Helen Reason

Printed by WS Bookwell

ISBN 1-85345-225-4

A Note from Ishmael

From an early age we Christians have been encouraged to believe that the Bible is the best book in the world. We claim that reading it brings us closer to God and most would go so far as to say that if we were stuck on a desert island and could only take one possession with us, we would choose to take our Bible. This of course all sounds very good, but is it true?

Nowadays I rarely see adults taking their Bibles to church meetings. I see children encouraged far more to read other books than they are encouraged to read their Bibles and, tragically, the day of people spending even a few minutes each day in their homes reading Scripture and praying together has long since gone.

Hey, this can't be right! Surely we all need to read the Bible, we all need to spend time praying and talking together and we all need to memorise Scripture.

I believe it's time to bring the daily devotional time back into the Christian home, and that is why I have written this simple 365-day devotional book, and released the 52-track Scripture song CD to accompany it.

Let me explain how it works ...

Firstly, I have not divided the book into specific months, so that you can start it at any time of the year.

Every day I begin with a Bible reading. May I suggest that if possible, rather than reading the verse from the book, take it in turns to find it and read it from a Bible so everyone begins to learn where the books can be found. This is where you will need both patience and the index! Following the reading, you will then see that I have made a few comments about the verse, sometimes a bit of teaching, sometimes a personal story, but either way it usually ends with something for us to prayerfully think about.

“” Then we pray a short prayer together.

After this we can have fun as we all contribute to the discussion point that I have added each day. ?

The minimum time this should take is five minutes which I'd hope all of us should be able to find in a day, but once we start praying and discussing, we can make that last as long as we want.

Every Sunday corresponds with the song and track order from my *52 Scripture Songs with Ishmael* album, so I am hoping that as we usually have more free time on Sundays, we can use some of this time to listen to the track and to learn the Bible verse off by heart. We can test each other every day throughout the following week to see if we still remember it. Just think how many Bible verses we will know by Week 52!

There are also a few days at the back of the book with special readings for Good Friday, Easter Day and Christmas Day.

Well, that's about it.

I hope you enjoy the book and, even more importantly, I pray God speaks to you as you spend time with Him and with each other each day.

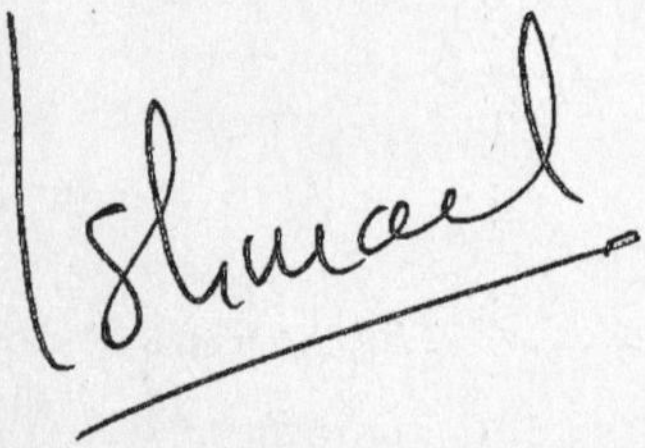

SUN

CD 1: 1

All Scripture is God-breathed ... (2 Tim. 3:16)

This is very exciting. Over this year, we will be spending a few minutes of each day together learning more about the Bible and what it has to teach us today. As we begin, we can see from our reading that the Bible (or Scriptures) is like no other book that has ever existed. This Book was written over a period of about 2,100 years, it has within its pages 66 smaller books and was written by at least 37 different authors. It is by far the best-selling book of all time, which is hardly surprising as this is God's Book and everything in it has been inspired by Him. Each day God wants to speak to us. As we read our verses together, let's make sure that we are always ready to listen to what He has to say.

Lord, thank You for Your Book, the Bible.

Do I believe all the Bible is true?

MON

A man of many companions may come to ruin, but there is a friend ... closer than a brother. (Prov. 18:24)

The best friend we can ever find is the Lord Jesus, but it's important to have other friends as well. Over the years many people have claimed to be my friends, but after a while I've discovered that they only wanted to be my friend for what they could get from me and, when I needed their help, they were never around! Thankfully not all friends are like that. Real close friends like us for who we are, not for what we have; they even put up with us when we get moody or bad-tempered. Good friends can be hard to come by, so when we find true friends let's try and keep them.

Lord, thank You for all the good friends around us, please help us to treat them in the same way that we like to be treated.

Who is my best friend?

TUES

"Peace I leave with you; my peace I give you." (John 14:27)

Problems, problems and yet more problems! I read the newspaper today and it seems like the world we live in is getting worse by the minute and that we are surrounded by troubled and confused men, women, boys and girls. We Christians must pray for those around us that God will help them. We must also realise that Jesus has given us a peace of heart and mind so that we need not be dragged down by the problems we all face. We have been given all we need to live like the victorious people that Jesus wants us to be.

Lord when problems come, help us to look to You, not just at the problems.

What is my major problem at the moment?

WEDS

We live by faith, not by sight. (2 Cor. 5:7)

Eyes are very important – it's very hard to see where we are going without them, although some wonderful people who have lost their sight do manage incredibly well. We Christians, however, do not just live by what our eyes can see, we live by what the Bible says. That is why we believe that impossible things can be made possible thanks to the Lord Jesus. Faith is believing that God is going to do something before it happens and before we can see it with our eyes.

Lord, please give us more faith today.

Is there an impossible thing I can see happening?

THURS

Fathers, do not exasperate your children ... (Eph. 6:4)

"It's only a bit of fun," we parents say, as we tease and "wind up" our children, "surely they have to learn to take a joke!" The trouble is, we adults don't always know when to stop. We can often see the anger and frustration rising up in our children as we continue to provoke them but we carry on, thinking it's all a laugh. Sadly, it usually ends with the children losing their temper and us punishing them for something that we should be punished for. So does this let children off the hook? Certainly not! Children often enjoy "winding up" their parents especially when they reach those wonderful teenage years! Humour is a gift from God, but not when it is at each other's expense.

Lord, help us never to deliberately make our children or parents angry by making fun of them.

Do we make each other angry?

FRI

Let the word of Christ dwell in you richly ... as you sing ... spiritual songs ... to God. (Col. 3:16)

I believe that music is a wonderful gift from God and a great way to be able to express our praise to Him. Music can also be used in other ways. Singing Scripture is a great way to remember the Word of God. I have deliberately linked this book with the *52 Scripture Songs* CD hoping that people would really try and learn a Scripture verse every week. The Scripture verses for every Sunday over the 52 weeks are on the CD and in the correct track order, so we will be able to both study the Bible verse, sing it and learn it off by heart. The verses we learn will be a great help to us as we live for Jesus, but we may need to sing them to remember them!

Lord, help us to memorise verses from the Bible.

How many Bible verses can I quote without opening my Bible?

SAT

The earth is the Lord's, and everything in it, the world, and all who live in it. (Psa. 24:1)

As I look out of my window, what do I see? I see litter covering my street, sad people passing by, obscene graffiti on the walls; I can smell polluting fumes and can see and hear police cars zooming by with sirens screeching. It's hard to imagine that all this belongs to the Lord. The evil one thinks he owns things and people, but how wrong he is. He does bring mess, chaos and destruction and he does ruin people's lives, but he will never own anything or anybody. Almighty God made the world and us, and He is still the owner of all the universe.

Lord, this is Your earth, please help us to do our best to look after it for You.

How can I help to make God's earth a better place?

Week 2

SUN

CD 1: 2

Jesus Christ is the same yesterday and today and for ever. (Heb. 13:8)

The seasons change, political parties change, even football rules and regulations change – I remember when you could fairly "shoulder barge" an opposing player without getting a red card! But, most of all, people are always changing and, sadly, not always for the better. In a world that is full of change it's great to know that our Lord Jesus will never change. Everything He said and everything He promised will last forever, and that includes His love for you and me. So if we are feeling let down, lonely or unloved let's take our eyes off changing people, and keep our eyes on the never-changing Lord Jesus.

Lord, we are so pleased that You constantly love us and that that will never change.

What is the greatest change that I have seen?

MON

The name of the Lord is a strong tower; the righteous run to it and are safe. (Prov. 18:10)

Ever felt a bit insecure? Ever thought that people are saying nasty things about you behind your back? Ever considered running away and hiding somewhere? If the answer's yes, it's time to run and get protection in that strong tower otherwise known as the Lord. Are there any conditions to enter that strong tower? Just one: we need to be people who try to do what is right, so that may mean a bit of confession before we enter. It's only when we get things right with God that we can know the security of living in that strong tower and not be scared about anything that is happening or anything that is being said by those around us.

Lord, make us clean inside and thank You for keeping us safe, like in a strong tower.

What makes me feel insecure?

TUES

... who satisfies your desires with good things so that your youth is renewed like the eagle's. (Psa. 103:5)

Even the very youngest of us will one day grow old. Today some of us may be getting old in years while others of us may not be old, but often feel it. I'm getting on a bit myself and although my mind never lets me believe I am getting old, my body keeps reminding me that I am no longer a spring chicken! I love today's verse; not only does God satisfy me with good things, which He does, but He also keeps me feeling young even if He does not keep me looking young! So as we all grow older, let's remember there is no need for us to feel old. We are going to live forever so putting time into eternity we all are really mere youngsters!

Lord, thank You for keeping us young.

If I could stay at one age, what age would I choose?

WEDS Be imitators of God ... (Eph. 5:1)

Who are we trying to be like today? Maybe when we got up we dressed really cool trying to copy the fashion of our favourite singer or film star. Maybe at work or school we try and imitate someone who is always popular. If we find time to kick a football around, we pretend we are the best player in the world. This is all part of life and growing up and, if we are honest, deep down we know we will never really be like any of these people, because we are us. However, there is one person we should imitate, and this person we can grow to be more like – the Lord Jesus. I wonder if those around us can see anything of Jesus in us today?

Lord, please help us to be more like You.

Who would I like to be like?

THURS From the rising of the sun to the place where it sets, the name of the Lord is to be praised. (Psa. 113:3)

Whatever the weather is like now, let's think of sunny summer mornings for a minute. When I was young, on the first day of summer, people from many different churches in our town would drive into the countryside at the rising of the dawn and there together we would have a great time praising God. It's a shame it only happened on one day a year. Perhaps in holiday time or at weekends we should go outside and praise God as we watch the dawn rise. We could even be more adventurous and maybe have a picnic breakfast as we do so. There is nothing quite like praising God early in the morning!

Lord, help us to start every day by praising You wherever we are.

What would stop me getting up early to praise God?

FRI

We ask you, brothers, to respect those ... over you in the Lord and who admonish you. (1 Thess. 5:12)

It's easy to criticise and complain about our church leaders. We seem to think that they should be perfect, work seven days a week, twenty-four hours a day and live on less money than we would want to live on. Our leaders have a tough and often thankless task. Just like us, they are human beings, sinners, and also like us often say and do things they shouldn't. However, with all their faults and failings, they have been called by God to lead and teach us. We should respect, love and encourage them; their lives are hard enough without us adding to the pressure and burdens they carry.

Lord, remind us to constantly say things to our leaders to encourage them.

What do I really think of my church leaders?

SAT

"My sheep listen to my voice; I know them, and they follow me." (John 10:27)

I spent some of my early years in farming and in my opinion some of the most stupid animals I ever had to look after were sheep. They would never listen to sensible instructions, they were scared of their own shadows and they would always follow other silly sheep even if they were heading for danger. They could not look after themselves and if a pregnant ewe ended up on her back, she would stay there and die unless the shepherd came along and saved her. Why on earth did Jesus ever liken you and me to these helpless, senseless animals. Hmmm, I think that is obvious!

Lord, thank You for caring for silly sheep like us.

What do I have in common with sheep?

SUN

CD 1: 3

The Lord will guide you always; he will satisfy your needs in a sun-scorched land. (Isa. 58:11)

I often look at my possessions that are cluttering up our house and think it's time for a big clear-out. Then I make excuses why I need to keep them. Some I need to keep because they have sentimental value and memories and I'd feel guilty about passing them on. Some I need to keep for a "rainy day" just in case they come in handy, but they probably never will. Some I need to keep to pass onto my kids one day, but will they really want them? God has promised to supply all my needs and maybe it's time to get rid of some of my old possessions to make room for the new He has lined up for me.

Lord, help us to store up real treasure, not junk.

What do I consider is junk and what is treasure?

MON

Is any one of you in trouble? He should pray. (James 5:13a)

I often wake up saying "Another day – another challenge", with things on my mind that are troubling me. Then I have to make a choice. Am I going spend the whole day letting these troubles buzz around inside my head or am I going to take notice of today's reading? I need to stop rushing around for a few minutes and tell the Lord about what's worrying me, and then leave these problems with Him. Jesus is happy to take these burdens from me and in their place leave a peace that He has reserved just for those who follow Him.

Lord, please sort out anything that is troubling us today.

What is troubling me today?

TUES

Is anyone happy? Let him sing songs of praise.

(James 5:13b)

Yesterday we learned that when we are having troubles we should pray. Today I hope we are feeling happy. Although life is never perfect, perhaps things are beginning to work out and we have a smile on our face and a spring in our step. I wonder how often we think of the Lord when we are happy or do we tend to only think of Him in our difficult times when we need something from Him? Let's not forget that the Lord also wants to be included in our happy times, so come on, let's sing a praise song to Him, or if we don't like singing, let's thank Him for the happiness that we are feeling today.

Lord, thank You for happiness.

What makes me happy?

WEDS

And my God will meet all your needs according to his glorious riches in Christ Jesus. (Phil. 4:19)

Does this mean that we will never be poor, hungry or in need of anything again? Is Paul saying that God must give us everything we ask for? Ah no. A few verses earlier Paul says that he has learned to be just as happy when he is poor, hungry and does not have all his needs met. Paul is just happy because he belongs to Jesus and he knows that Jesus will never let him down – even if he has to go through hard times or sometimes go without. There is no one richer than Jesus, and when we really know Him, we also realise that there is no one richer than we are.

Lord, even if we don't have a lot of money, thank You for making us so rich.

How am I rich?

THURS

As far as the east is from the west, so far has he removed our transgressions from us. (Psa. 103:12)

Q) Is anyone feeling guilty today? A) Yes. Q) Why do we keep on saying, doing and thinking things which we know are wrong? A) I don't know. Q) If we are truly sorry for these wrong things and ask Jesus to forgive us, will He? A) Yes, He not only forgives us, but He also separates our sin from us as far as anything could be separated. Q) How far is that? A) As far as the east is from the west. Q) And how far is that? A) It's so far that nobody could ever calculate it. Wow!

“” **Lord, thank You for forgiving us and separating us from everything we do that's wrong.**

? **Do I really believe all my past sins have been separated from me?**

FRI

Shout for joy ... the Lord comforts his people and will have compassion on his afflicted ones. (Isa. 49:13)

There are times when we all feel bad. We may be suffering in our minds, or in our bodies. There are times when we all feel very sad because one of our loved ones or friends has recently died. It's in times like these that we need people to encourage, comfort and pray for us even though the pain or hurt may still remain. Earthly friends can be a great source of help, but nobody can comfort us like our Heavenly Father and He is the only one who, in time, can turn our sadness to joy.

“” **Lord, please comfort us and all others that need comforting today.**

? **Which earthly person would I go to for comfort?**

SAT

"And do not set your heart on what you will eat or drink; do not worry about it." (Luke 12:29)

I am sure there is something wrong with my scales and why do I look so fat every time I look at myself in the mirror? OK, the diet definitely starts tomorrow. Tonight I will spend hours shopping, examining the labels on the tins and only buying food that has very few calories; but we must not keep thinking about food and drink, says Jesus in our reading. Of course exercise and a reasonably healthy diet are important, but there are so many more important issues that should be filling our minds other than worrying about what goes in our mouths.

Lord, help us to concentrate on the important issues in life.

Am I worried about my weight?

Week 4

SUN

CD 1: 4

"If you have faith as small as a mustard seed ... say ... 'Be uprooted ...,' and it will obey you." (Luke 17:6)

A mustard seed is tiny. I am sure that whatever age we are, every one of us believers has that amount of faith, although I think we may have needed more faith than that when we first became Christians. The problem is, often we are too scared to put our faith into action. God wants both young and old to do impossible things to give glory to Jesus. This will demand faith, and we should never be frightened to step out in this faith when Jesus tells us to.

Lord, help us not to be frightened to step out in faith and ask You to do the impossible.

How much faith do I have?

MON

The eyes of all look to you, and you give them their food at the proper time. (Psa. 145:15)

Even as I write this I am feeling a bit hungry. I am one of these people who can literally eat anything … and enjoy it, which is why I will never be thin. It does annoy me slightly when I see people picking over food and complaining, especially as we know that God supplies us with so many good things to eat while many people in the world are hungry and do not have the choice that we have. Next time we walk around a large food store, let's be grateful that every meal is not just plain rice, and let's stop complaining about the food that is set before us.

Lord, thank You for giving us such a choice of food.

What is my favourite food?

TUES

After they prayed, the place where they were meeting was shaken. (Acts 4:31)

Sadly today, the worst attended meeting in most of our churches is the prayer meeting. So often it is just a few people sitting for an hour talking to God but never really expecting to "feel the walls shake". In our church the young people began something called 24/7. For this they took over a room and manned it with at least two people praying for 24 hours a day 7 days a week. They found prayer so exciting they did not want to stop, and kept going for weeks. Prayer meetings may not be exciting, but real prayer always is!

Lord, help us to see how exciting prayer really is.

Do I enjoy praying?

WEDS

Submit yourselves for the Lord's sake to every authority instituted among men. (1 Pet. 2:13)

Do we ever feel that we can do what we like so long as we don't sin? We can break the speed limits, fiddle our taxes, park illegally, ride our bikes in pedestrian areas and even cheat in exams. Surely it's OK so long as we don't get caught, and God won't mind ... or will He? We are told to obey those who lay down the laws and God is not happy with us when we don't. The only exception would be if people in authority tried to force us to do things which the Bible says are wrong, but I don't think the things I included above fit into that category. We must remember, most laws are put into place for the good and safety of us and others.

“” **Lord, help us to obey the laws laid down by those in authority.**

? **Do I break any laws?**

THURS

Bear with each other and forgive whatever grievances you may have against one another. (Col. 3:13)

Yes, I know people have said and done some awful things to you. Would you believe me if I told you that I (and probably everyone else in the world) have been through similar hurtful experiences at one time or another? But we Christians must react differently to many around us. When someone is horrible to us, we should not want revenge, we should want to forgive the person who hurt us and win back their friendship. I know it sounds hard, maybe impossible, but if that is what Jesus wants us to do, if we cannot do it, are we really His followers?

“” **Lord, help us to forgive others.**

? **Who has hurt me?**

FRI

As the rain and the snow come down from heaven ... without watering the earth ... (Isa. 55:10)

We all may complain about different things, but most of us complain about the rain. We do not like getting wet and rain stops us from getting outdoors and doing the things that we enjoy doing. If we wake up hearing raindrops on our windows it sometimes makes us feel downright depressed. But let's not forget, it's God who sends the rain, it is not a wicked act from the evil one. The flowers, crops and vegetables cry out for rain and, let's face it, we would not survive for long without it either. However, rain may be God-sent but personally, living in the UK, I would appreciate a little more sun to balance things out.

Lord, next time it rains help us not to complain, but to thank You for sending it.

What do I think of rainy weather?

SAT

For he has rescued us from the dominion of darkness ...

(Col. 1:13)

I remember in my younger days when I was a pastor in Lancashire the youth group encouraged me to go potholing with them in a lovely place called Ingleton. Once undergound in the caves we were all told to turn off the lights on our helmets and then for the first time I realised what true darkness was really like. Even as a man I would have been scared to be left in that darkness alone. As Christians we can still feel the presence of spiritual darkness but we should never be frightened by it because Jesus, the light of the world, has set us free from the power of it. We now live in the light with Jesus.

Lord, thank You that spiritual darkness will never control us again.

Do I feel under the control of anything bad?

SUN

CD 1: 5

And the child grew and became strong ... filled with wisdom, and the grace of God ... (Luke 2:40)

It's hard to imagine Jesus as a little boy, running around and playing games, having friends, enjoying times of happiness and facing times of sadness. One of the reasons for this is because the Bible tells us so little about those early years. As He grew, so He became strong, probably by helping Joseph carry large pieces of wood around. But there was one thing that made Him different from any other child that has ever lived, He never did one thing wrong. He was the perfect child in every way.

Lord, help us to do all we can to make sure all children have a happy childhood.

How can I make children I know happy?

MON

Teach me to do your will, for you are my God. (Psa. 143:10)

I spend a lot of my time with boys and girls, and usually when I meet them they tend to be on their best behaviour. I also am a dad, and I remember when my children were small that there would be times when they would fight and argue to try and get their own way. As a Christian adult, I still sometimes act like a naughty child and argue with Father God, stupidly thinking that I know best. God has sorted out the best possible life for me and I need to learn to do what He wants me to do without argument.

Lord, teach us to do Your will.

What do I enjoy arguing about?

TUES

Without weakening in his faith, he faced the fact that ... he was about a hundred years old. (Rom. 4:19)

We may only be as old as we feel, but how old are we feeling today? Some of us would say very old and life is passing us by. Wait a minute, at a hundred years old Abraham was still considering the prospect of fatherhood again. In some ways life was just beginning for him. Even if we have reached one hundred years young, perhaps we should stop worrying about getting old and treat every day as a new adventure with new challenges to overcome and accomplish. A Christian never retires from obeying and following Jesus.

“” **Lord, thank You that life is always an adventure.**

? **Do I believe in retirement?**

WEDS

"I have loved you with an everlasting love." (Jer. 31:3)

Some of those TV "soaps" are so unreal. We hear two 15-year-olds saying they are madly in love with each other, yet two weeks later they have both fallen in love with someone else! The Greek language helpfully had a few words for "love" whereas we have just got the one. Love is a very deep feeling and I don't believe it should be taken lightly. Sadly many adults who really do fall in love, at a later date fall out of love through various, sometimes very tragic circumstances. The best news for a Christian is that God's love never changes, and His love for us will last forever.

“” **Lord, it's great to know that You will always love us.**

? **What does love mean to me?**

THURS "Come down from the cross and save yourself!" (Mark 15:30)

Jesus was hanging from a cross in total agony. He was all alone because his friends had left Him, and even Father God had to look away as He took all our sin into Himself. As if that were not bad enough, He also had the religious leaders shouting insults at Him and making fun of Him. Jesus only had to give the word and angels would have shot down from the heavens and destroyed everyone, but if He'd done that, there would have been no way for you or I to have our sins forgiven and to be made right with God.

Lord, thank You.

What do I think about people wearing crucifixes or crosses around their necks?

FRI "Now that I, your Lord and Teacher, have washed your feet ... wash one another's feet." (John 13:14)

At times we all, whether we are young or old, can feel full of our own self-importance and treat others as less important. The truth is that none of us are important, but through Jesus dying for us He has made us all very special. That of course means everyone including children. Adults, we must be very careful that we never look down on little ones. I have seen children treated like slaves, being ordered to do this and that without even getting a please and thank you. Whatever age we are, we all need to make each other feel special, by humbling ourselves and "washing each other's feet".

Lord, please help us to be humble.

Can I think of anyone who I treat as less important than me?

SAT

Lord, you establish peace for us; all that we have accomplished you have done for us. (Isa. 26:12)

We do not like failing do we, it's humiliating and often brings our self-worth right down. However, it's even harder for us Christians to cope with success. Pride is a hard sin to deal with because we all want to believe that our successes are due to our own capabilities and achievements. Every success we experience is due to Jesus and we must give Him all the credit and praise for everything. If we choose not to, we may still carry on being successful in our own eyes and in the eyes of those around us, but that adds up to nothing if our relationship with Jesus has been broken.

Lord, thank You for every success in our lives.

What are my failures and successes?

Week 6

SUN

CD 1: 6

Whatever you do, work at it with all your heart, as working for the Lord, not for men. (Col. 3:23)

Have you noticed, if we enjoy doing a job or some schoolwork we throw ourselves into it wholeheartedly? If we don't enjoy it, we just do the bare necessity that requires the least amount of effort. I find this verse a great challenge because, whatever I do, I should try and imagine that I am doing it to please Jesus, not just the people or teachers around me. This would then mean that I am going to do the very best I can with everything I put my hand to. We live in an age where anything will do so we Christians should be an example so that however menial the task, people can expect the very best from us.

Lord, whatever we do, help us to put all our effort into it.

What jobs do I hate doing?

MON

The Lord is not slow in keeping his promise ... (2 Pet. 3:9)

I have sometimes been talking to someone and discovered that although they are nodding their head, they are not listening to a word I am saying. Prayer is so wonderful, because when we talk to our Heavenly Father, He always listens to us, and He always answers us. Sometimes when His answers are not instant, we may think that He is not interested in what we are saying, that's not so. God is always interested in us, and when He says He will do something, He will definitely do it, but in His time not ours.

Lord, thank You that You always listen to us.

Do I listen to people when they talk to me?

TUES

But now ... we have been released from the law ... (Rom. 7:6)

Of course we know we must obey the laws of our land, but must we still obey all the laws in the Bible? In Old Testament times the law was vital to teach people what sin was and how bad people were, compared to a holy God. In New Testament times Jesus taught that we can no longer be made good by keeping the law, but by believing in Him and living lives that please Him. Now we have no excuses. Jesus has fixed it so that we are no longer prisoners to the law or to sin. We no longer live by written rules, we Christians are now in a love relationship with a Saviour who really cares for us. We must never forget that, although we may not be perfect yet, Jesus still wants us to be holy.

Lord, we know we are free, help us to be holy.

Can I think of any Old Testament laws that are still laws in our country today?

WEDS

Two are better than one, because they have a good return for their work. (Eccl. 4:9)

I love walking around our local golf course, with its beautiful lakes, lush green grass, birds singing, rabbits hopping around; in fact the only thing that is not beautiful is my golf! I don't care though, it's a great chance to be alone to think and to pray. But I have not been called to be a monk and isolated. I need to be with others for friendship, for accountability and also for ministry. I guess that is why Jesus sent out His disciples in twos. More can be done when two of us work together. Have we all got a close friend to be alongside us? It's better if we have.

Lord, thank You for those who share in our life.

Who is my closest Christian friend?

THURS

Why are you downcast, O my soul? Why so disturbed within me? Put your hope in God ... (Psa. 43:5)

There is nothing wrong with being sad or upset. Some people, especially men and boys, think tears are a sign of weakness. I remember when my Dad died I could not stop crying and quite wrongly felt very embarrassed by this. However, although we will all experience times of sadness, we are not called to live a life of sadness. We are victorious conquerors, living in the joy of our Lord. And what's the best way to cheer ourselves up? Easy, think how great God is ... and keep praising Him.

Lord, please turn our sadness into joy.

How do I cheer myself up?

FRI

"Can a mother forget the baby at her breast ... See, I have engraved you on ... my hands." (Isa. 49:15-16)

Irene and I have three wonderful children. Of course they are now grown-up, but they are still just as wonderful to us as they were when they were little. I, being the brave father I am, was there at each birth, but being the coward I am, nearly fainted at each one. I cannot stand the sight of blood! But I will never forget those birth days, and I am sure that Irene definitely won't! Father God will never forget us, He has our names written on His hand, He knew us long before our births and there is no one who could know us better, or love us more than He does.

Lord, it's great to know that You will never forget us.

Are there people I have forgotten who I should be remembering?

SAT

He said to them, "Go into all the world and preach the good news to all creation." (Mark 16:15)

This sounds exciting. Jesus wants me to go to all the different countries in the world and tell them about Him. I think I will start in the Bahamas then go to Africa, then ... hold on before you buy your air ticket, I do not think that is quite what He meant.
For some, "the world" will mean to travel overseas, but that is not the same for everyone. Jesus wants us to pass on His good news to the world around us, and that means where we live, in our school, at the shops and where we work. I know it may not sound quite so exciting, but when one of our friends decides to follow Jesus, that is even more exciting than a trip to the Bahamas!

Lord, help us to share Your good news to all those in our world.

Let me tell you about my world.

SUN

CD 1: 7

God saw all that he had made, and it was very good. (Gen. 1:31)

Imagine God making bright light, total darkness, the burning sun, the mighty oceans, beautiful flowers and every type of animal, fish and bird. What fun He must have had. When He had finished, He stopped and looked at what He had made and He saw how good it was. But although all creation was good, God's masterpiece was man, because He made man in His own image. As we look at our bodies and how God made them work we are fascinated. As we consider how God created our minds, brains and emotions we are amazed. As we look at the part of us that is going to live forever with Jesus, we are so grateful.

Lord, everything You made is so good, thank You.

What is my favourite animal?

MON

"I have not come to call the righteous, but sinners to repentance." (Luke 5:32)

I have met some people who really believe that they are not sinners because they have never murdered anyone or robbed a bank. Even more people believe that children cannot be sinners because they are only young. According to the Bible, however, we are all sinners because even if we think we do not *do* very bad things, we all *think* bad things, and according to Jesus that is still sin. But this is not all bad news. Being a sinner means that I am one of the people that Jesus loves, and it's only the people who admit they're sinners who are given the opportunity to change and become much better people. The best news of all is, the more I become like Jesus, the less of a sinner I will be.

Lord, please help each of us to be less of a sinner and more like You.

What sin keeps tempting me the most?

TUES

For whoever finds me finds life and receives favour from the Lord.

(Prov. 8:35)

Life's not so bad is it, I mean with all the hardships and problems we face, we still manage to laugh and find something to be happy about. Maybe there is a new little baby born in the family, maybe it's the thought of our favourite sports team doing well, or maybe it's that our holidays are not far away. So if we are thinking that life is good, it gets a whole lot better once we find Jesus. You see Jesus not only gives those who love Him the best life possible, but He really is what living is all about.

Lord, thank You that You are not just the provider of happiness, You are the provider of real life.

What makes life good?

WEDS

The end of a matter is better than its beginning. (Eccl. 7:8)

I know we all do it, but it is not good. Maybe it's a job in the house or garden that needs doing, maybe it's tidying our bedrooms, usually it's something that needs some attention which we don't want to do. We start something ... then we give up on it and start doing something else. When we begin something we need to keep going until we finish it. Paul in the Bible talks about the Christian life as though it is a race; once we have started, we must not give up, even if we feel tired and have blisters on our feet. There is a great satisfaction in completing a job and an even greater satisfaction in our walk with Jesus in keeping going till the finishing line.

Lord, we have started following You, please help us to never give up.

What jobs are waiting for me to finish?

THURS

Do not be quickly provoked in your spirit, for anger resides in the lap of fools. (Eccl. 7:9)

I know we must love everybody, but there are some people who always manage to offend and upset us. When they annoy us, it does not take long for our anger to build up and soon we have reacted and said something to them that was very unkind and wrong. For a short while we may feel quite pleased with ourselves, we have let that person have "a piece of our mind", but then in time we think how foolish we have been, we have not acted like Christians who are following Jesus. If we have acted in this way, there is nothing else for it, we must say sorry even if the other person never does.

Lord, help us not to get angry, and when we do, to be able to say we're sorry.

What makes me angry?

FRI

"I tell you the truth, he who believes has everlasting life." (John 6:47)

When I was young I never worried about dying. I thought that I would live forever and the way that I rode motorbikes, drove cars and did crazy stunts proved that. Now that I am way past the halfway mark of my three score years and ten, I often think about what is going to happen when I die. The great news about being a Christian is that I believe everything that Jesus said is true. He promised that if I believe in Him, and live my life for Him, although I may die I will spend forever with Him. I can't go wrong being a Christian. While alive on earth, I get the best life possible, and when I die I get an even better life which lasts forever. Wow!

Lord, thank You that we are going to live forever.

What do I think I will be doing in heaven?

SAT

God made him who had no sin to be sin for us ... (2 Cor. 5:21)

I do love watching biblical epic movies. Of course very few can be accurate scripturally as the violence and adult "happenings" would make them all rated "18" and even then certain scenes would have to be censored. I think the worst thing about these films, however, are the actors who try and portray Jesus. They must be good-looking with perfect bodies and hairstyles to match. The Bible tells us that Jesus was nothing special to look at, in fact He was probably quite ordinary. What made Him stand out from every other human being that has ever lived was that He was perfect ... He never sinned once ... He was totally pure in every way. Amazing and wonderful.

Lord, we sin, You never did, please make us more like You.

Which story in the Bible would I most like to see made into a good film?

Week 8

SUN

CD 1: 8

Sing to God, sing praise to his name ... (Psa. 68:4–6)

As I travel I get to hear all types of people singing their praises to God. I have heard large choirs who sound majestic but very rarely smile. I have heard soloists with the most wonderfully trained voices but whose faces never seem to show that they are enjoying praising. I have watched rock singers who always look serious when they are praising God because that is the cool thing to do. I have also met children, some who may never sing in a choir, be soloists or rock singers ... but you can see by their happy smiling faces that they are really enjoying praising God. You can guess who I enjoy watching and listening to the most can't you!

Lord, help our faces to show that we enjoy singing praises to God.

Which Christian singers do I most enjoy listening to?

MON

Finally, be strong in the Lord and in his mighty power. (Eph. 6:10)

When I was younger I fancied having a body bulging with rippling muscles. I joined a gym and regularly tried out all the weight machines, but as I looked in the mirror after a few weeks, sadly, I looked just the same. I even bought a muscle expander and even though it was guaranteed to do the business, it failed on me! I felt like writing to the manufacturer who gave that guarantee and telling them that I had bought their gadget, could they now please send me some muscles! Nowadays I realise that yes, I need to be strong, but strong in the Lord, and the only way to achieve "spiritual muscles" is not in the gym but by reading my Bible regularly and spending time talking and listening to God.

Lord, help us to be strong as Christians.

Do I enjoy reading the Bible regularly?

TUES

Be still before the Lord and wait patiently for him. (Psa. 37:7)

The worst thing about taking exams is that you do not get the results immediately. I would do my best under the pressure of the exam room and then, as I walked out of the door, I would feel even more stressed as I knew I would have to wait for ages before I would know if I had passed or failed. In the Christian life we love to rush into things without even consulting Jesus. We think, "God has given us brains, let's just get on and use them." Of course sometimes this may be right, but I am learning that while patiently waiting for God's guidance may not come naturally to me, I make less mistakes when I do so.

Lord, teach us to be patient and to wait for Your guidance.

Do I think that I am a patient person?

WEDS

What man can live and not see death, or save himself from the power of the grave? (Psa. 89:48)

When the psalmist wrote this, there were no options. Everyone was going to die sooner or later. Nowadays, sadly, people still die, but Jesus promised that there will be a time when some people won't. Some day soon Jesus will leave His Father in heaven and will come back to earth and take all those who love Him to be with Him forever and they will not die. Of course nobody knows the exact day or date when Jesus will return, but one thing we can be sure of, it is a lot closer now than it was in the day of the disciples. We must stay prepared and close to Jesus, He could return at any time and it is sure to be when we least expect it.

" **Lord, help us to be prepared on the day You come back to earth.**

? **How far away do I think the Lord's return is?**

THURS

Dear children, do not let anyone lead you astray. (1 John 3:7)

When I was about 11 years old, one of my school friends offered me a cigarette. I really had no desire to puff on the weed, but in those days it was the trendy thing for people my age to do. For a while I refused, but as all my friends were smoking and constantly inviting me to join them, I eventually gave in and was soon starting down the addiction road along with everyone else. It is very easy to be encouraged by others to take part in things that we really do not want to do. What they choose to do is up to them, but we must learn to stand firm and to say no.

" **Lord, help us not to be led into things that we do not want to do.**

? **What wrong things have people tried to make me do?**

FRI

For though we live in the world, we do not wage war as the world does. (2 Cor. 10:3)

Most weeks we can watch the news and see rival football fans at war with each other, or walk through our town centres and see drunken people throwing their fists around trying to hurt anyone within their range. Some people seem to feel good about fighting and injuring other people but we Christians should have no time for violence. We will all meet aggressive people but we are here to show them love, not to show them how strong we are. If we need proof of this, we just need to look again at the arrest of Jesus: the bullies beat Him up terribly, but His only retaliation was to forgive them.

Lord, help us not to be aggressive.

What makes me want to fight?

SAT

If we confess our sins, he is faithful and just and will forgive us our sins. (1 John 1:9)

There is one thing that the old and young and the rich and poor have in common – they all sin. God set a standard that He wanted people to live up to, but starting with Adam and Eve and continued by you and me, we have all fallen well short of the standard that God set. Still, it's not all bad news. If we confess our sin and say sorry to God, the great news is that He not only forgives us, but completely wipes our wrongdoing from His memory banks. A bit of advice though, let's not store up saying sorry until the end of the week or even the end of the day, we must try and say sorry as soon as we recognise that we have done wrong.

Lord, help us to say sorry immediately we do wrong things.

When did I last say sorry to God?

SUN

CD 1: 9

Children, obey your parents in the Lord, for this is right ... (Eph. 6:1–2)

No parents are perfect. All parents sometimes make the wrong decisions and sometimes say the wrong things, and all parents at sometime or other treat their children really badly. But even after saying all this, the Bible does say that the right thing for children to do is to obey their parents. Let's never forget though, like husband and wife, it is a two-way relationship. I believe the more parents show real love, respect and attention to their children the more obedience they will get in return.

Lord, help us to be more obedient to You, and as children to be more obedient to our parents.

Do I enjoy obeying my parents?

MON

Clap your hands, all you nations ... (Psa. 47:1a)

We have all done it. Maybe at a concert, maybe at a sports event, or maybe when a member of the family has achieved something. We have congratulated them by putting both our hands together and making a noise! I would love to see it also happen more frequently in some of our meetings. Maybe after a good talk or a good time of praising God with the musicians. God loves us to encourage each other, and clapping is a good way to do this. But we can also clap our hands in appreciation of the Lord – it's great to show our thanks to people, but nobody deserves more thanks than God.

Lord, help us not to be scared to show our appreciation to both You and others by clapping.

When did I last clap my hands?

TUES ... shout to God with cries of joy.

(Psa. 47:1b)

Now if you have ever heard me sing, you will have realised that God did not bless me with an operatic or even a very sweet singing voice. God gifted me with the voice of a shouter, so I guess that is why I relate so well to today's Bible reading. Maybe one or two of you are like me but think the shouters are not quite as talented as the singers; well, we may not sound as tuneful but we are just as biblical. We all use our voices to shout encouragement to our favourite sports team and personalities, so it's even more important to use them to shout to the Lord because He is the One who brings joy into our lives.

Lord, help us not to be afraid to shout out our thanks to You.

When did I last shout?

WEDS He gives strength to the weary ...

(Isa. 40:29a)

According to one of my favourite cartoons of long ago, if I wanted strength I would get it from a tin of spinach, or so Popeye the sailor man assured me. Popeye would be in the most impossible situation when out of his shirt would appear a tin of spinach. (How many tins did he keep in there?) Suddenly, after a little tune and gulping down the spinach, his muscles were bulging everywhere and he would win the day. Nowadays if we want strength as a Christian, especially if we are feeling tired, it's not just food, pills or even sleep we need, we need to spend time with Jesus and He will renew our strength so that we too can do impossible things and win the day for God.

Lord, You give us strength when we need it.

What do I do when I am tired?

THURS ... and increases the power of the weak. (Isa. 40:29b)

Yesterday we looked at strength, today we look at the second part of the verse – at power. Powerful people can be very dangerous because some weaker people not only look up to them but are easily influenced by them. If the powerful person makes a wrong decision or turns bad it can have a devastating effect on the weaker follower. In church life it can be the same. Some Christians love power and being in control and this also is very dangerous. We should never seek power just so that we can be powerful. It's only the weak that will receive God's power and that's the only power we really should want in our lives.

“ ” **Lord, we are weak, please fill us with Your power.**

? **Who do I have any power over?**

FRI He got up, rebuked the wind and said to the waves, "Quiet! Be still!" (Mark 4:39)

I live fairly near the seaside and although it's lovely to sit on the beach in the summer when the sun is shining and the sea is warm, I really prefer to be on the beach in the winter. I love it when there is hardly anyone about, the wind is blowing and the waves are crashing down on the pebbles – because it reminds me of how powerful God is. And then I think of today's verse. As I look at the power and noise of God's creation I realise a word from Jesus can stop it all. Wind, be quiet, waves be still. This reminds me that Jesus has power over absolutely everything.

“ ” **Lord, thank You that You are in control of the whole world around us.**

? **Should I pray for the weather?**

SAT

The Lord is a warrior. (Exod. 15:3)

So often we think of the Lord as just gentle and kind, loving everyone, and Someone who always has time to listen to our prayers. Of course He is all these things, but we must not forget that He is also a warrior. He does not just sit around all day, He is fighting for truth and righteousness. He is with us to protect us when the evil one attacks and He shields us from many dangers. But, remember, He will never take away our free will, and if we choose to wander off from His protection we will have to face the consequences.

Lord, thank You for being a strong and mighty warrior.

Do I prefer to think of the Lord as a peacemaker or a warrior?

Week 10

SUN

CD 1: 10

I will take refuge in the shadow of your wings until the disaster has passed. (Psa. 57:1)

I think it's wonderful that even when a mother bird could be facing all sorts of traumas, the little baby chicks snuggle beneath her wings, oblivious of any fear that their mother may be feeling. They must feel so warm, secure and loved. This is just how God wants us to be with Him. We are not going to bury our head in the sand and ignore the storms, but when we see the storms approaching we will run to God who will protect us through them, and under His wings, we too will feel warm, secure and loved.

Lord, thank You that when we see the storm coming, the safest place to be is with You.

What is my favourite bird?

MON

"But after me will come one who is more powerful than I ... "

(Matt. 3:11)

John the Baptist was an amazing man sent to prepare the way of the Lord. Because he was a powerful preacher, he had his own followers and they thought that he must be the new Messiah sent from God. John soon put them right. "Another is coming who is more powerful than I am," he told them, "He is the one you should be looking out for." It's nice when people congratulate and admire us but let us never become proud. At every opportunity we need to remind people that there is someone far greater than us that they need to get to know – the Lord Jesus.

Lord, help us to always point people towards You.

Do I have followers? Who are they?

TUES

He fills his hands with lightning and commands it to strike its mark.

(Job 36:32)

Although some people may be a little afraid of lightning, it is one of God's most fantastic displays of power. Many years ago some of the leaders of a beautiful historic cathedral were making some comments that denied important truths in the Bible. One morning they awoke to discover that lightning had struck part of their precious building and set it on fire. Was this co-incidence or sent from heaven? Well, according to our Bible reading, God sometimes does seem to aim lightning at certain targets, which is both frightening and fantastic. We serve a powerful God who has all creation within His power.

Lord, thank You that lightning is another show of Your great power.

Am I scared of lightning?

WEDS

" ... the Lord Jesus himself said: 'It is more blessed to give than to receive.'" (Acts 20:35)

Whenever my birthday gets close, I still get a little excited about it, but for different reasons than when I was younger. When I was young the excitement revolved around the gifts I would receive, today it revolves around meeting up with the family and having fun together. But I enjoy celebrating other people's birthdays even more, and that has nothing to do with me getting old! I find it more fun to give a gift than to actually receive one. It's such a great joy watching people's faces as they receive a present that they were really hoping that they would get.

Lord, it's great to receive, but it's even better to give.

Do I prefer to give or receive?

THURS

Joseph stayed in Egypt, along with all his father's family. (Gen. 50:22)

All families go through rough patches, and none I guess more than Joseph's. His brothers had been jealous of him and wanted to kill him, but then decided instead to sell him as a slave. You would have thought that he would not want anything else to do with his family after being treated so badly. In fact the opposite was true. Even though his family had put him through such pain, he still loved them, forgave them and ended his days living with them. Let's not allow family feuds to get out of hand, let's learn from Joseph and try to keep a good relationship between family members, even if we are the innocent party.

Lord, help us to love our family at all times.

Have my family treated me badly?

FRI

Then he opened their minds so they could understand the Scriptures. (Luke 24:45)

Reading the Bible regularly is very important for us as Christians. A few years ago, everyone was told that they must have a "quiet time with their Bibles" every day, or else! Nowadays it's gone to the other extreme and many Christians hardly ever pick up their Bibles and prefer to spend their time listening to teaching and praise recordings rather than studying God's Word for themselves. Sometimes we read the Bible quickly just like a novel, which is fine, but to get the best from it we need to ask Jesus to "open our minds" so we really can understand all the wonderful treasures that are hidden within its pages.

Lord, please open our minds as we spend time reading the Bible.

How often do I read the Bible?

SAT

The apostles performed many miraculous signs and wonders among the people. (Acts 5:12)

Preaching the good news of Jesus is very important. Living a life that gives glory to Jesus is also very important. We hope our friends who are not yet Christians will listen to what we say, and look at the way we live. But there is a very important dynamic missing … the supernatural power of the Holy Spirit. One third of the Gospels are taken up with Jesus performing the impossible and nobody has ever walked the walk or talked the talk like Jesus. If Jesus knew that people needed to see signs and wonders to believe, how much more do you and I need to be asking God to use us in the miraculous in this day and age.

Lord, please help us to use signs and wonders to give glory to Your name.

What last sign or wonder did God use me in?

SUN

CD 1: 11

"Here I am! I stand at the door and knock." (Rev. 3:20)

I guess we have all had some "unwelcome" visitors knocking on our doors. I once had a loft insulation salesman standing on my doorstep insisting that my loft needed insulating, when at the time I was living in a house with a flat roof that had no loft! Jesus knocks at the door of our lives, but He will never push His way in, He waits patiently for us to open that door and welcome Him inside. Jesus will never leave us, but by leaving Him standing outside the door, we are treating Him like an unwelcome visitor that we don't want anything to do with. This must make Him very sad.

Lord, we want You to be with us always, we never want to shut You out of our lives.

Who would I not invite into my home?

MON

Since no man knows the future, who can tell him what is to come? (Eccl. 8:7)

Some people think that they can tell us the future through fortune-telling and horoscopes. As Christians we need to avoid both these people and their predictions. At best they are out to cheat us by lies, and at worst they may be involved with witchcraft which the Bible tells us is evil and bad. Although God knows what is going to happen in the future, no person does. Our lives are in His hands and we can be sure that whatever we have to face, He will be there to face it with us. Let's not worry about tomorrow too much, let's get on and enjoy the presence of God today.

Lord, help us live for You today and not worry about tomorrow.

Would I really like to know what the future holds?

TUES

Abstain from sinful desires, which war against your soul. (1 Pet. 2:11)

I don't think that I was a bad kid but I know there were times when I wanted my own way and my parents would not let me have it. My first response to this was to keep asking, then I'd pull a miserable face, and after that I'd make a sort of crying noise, but as no tears flowed, it was more a crying out of anger that I was not allowed to have my own way. Nowadays, I still at times desire things that Heavenly Father does not want me to have or do. The temptations are just as powerful and sometimes, sadly, I give in to them and have to say sorry, but the older I get the more I can see the wisdom in Heavenly Father's decisions. He only wants what is best for me.

Lord, please help us not to give in to sinful desires.

How do I try and get my own way?

WEDS

The Lord was with Samuel as he grew up ... (1 Sam. 3:19)

It is true that Samuel was an exceptional child – a miracle birth, given over to God at a very early age, and chosen by God to be one of the greatest prophets that has ever lived. I still meet people who think that children have no spiritual value until they become teenagers. Why don't these people read their Bibles! Just as the Lord was preparing Samuel from a very early age, so He is preparing our children. One of my greatest thrills is that I keep meeting people, now in their twenties, who became Christians at one of our meetings when they were very young and are now being mightily used by God. Those early years are as important to God as the later ones.

Lord, thank You that You also use little ones to help fulfil Your plans.

When was the last time I saw God use a child?

THURS

"Your servant has nothing at all," she said, "except a little oil." (2 Kings 4:2)

The poor widow was desperate with massive debt problems when she bumped into Elisha. When Elisha asked what she had, her reply was our Scripture verse. Nothing ... except. In other words she did not exactly have nothing, she had that little bit of oil which, by a miracle, God was going to multiply, and would be the answer to paying off all she owed. You and I may feel we have got nothing, but we always have a little something, and that something is just the thing that God can use to help us get out of our troubles.

Lord, thank You that You can make a lot out of very little.

What little something have I got that may be valuable?

FRI

Your beauty should not come from outward adornment ... (1 Pet. 3:3)

I know how long it takes for my wife and daughter to get ready if we are going out for the evening – a lot longer than it takes me. Now that is not a bad thing, I enjoy it when they walk out of the door all dressed up and looking great, but I do not love them any more than if they were wearing a pair of old jeans and a tee shirt. Paul says real beauty is not found in what we look like, it's found in our inner self. Sadly, many choose a partner just because they look good. If or when you are looking for a partner it is the inner person you need to fall in love with, not just the person that your eyes enjoy looking at.

Lord, thank You that we are surrounded by beautiful people.

What clothes do I most like wearing?

SAT

God said to Noah ... "So make yourself an ark ... " (Gen. 6:13–14)

Now it's unlikely that Noah knew what rain was, or that his garden backed onto the sea or a large river, so to be told to build a big boat would have been quite strange. He probably would have had to hire carpenters to come and help with the job. I wonder what they thought of Noah and the massive project. What people think, however, is not important. It's being obedient to God that is all important. I guarantee there will be times when God will ask us to do some strange things; like Noah, we must not worry about what other people think, we must go ahead and do them. Why? Because Almighty God has told us to.

Lord, help us to do all the things that You ask us to, however strange they may seem.

What strange things has God asked me to do?

Week 12

SUN

CD 1: 12

But I call to God, and the Lord saves me. (Psa. 55:16)

We all have difficult days when nothing seems to go right and we find ourselves feeling very distressed like David as he wrote this psalm. I think we can learn from how he dealt with his depressing situation. He called to the Lord morning, noon and night and God heard and answered his prayer. I wonder if we pray once, then give up and carry on living in misery for the rest of the day thinking that God is either too busy or is not interested in our situation? Let's keep praying, because in the end it is only God who can lift us out of our depressing day and put a smile back on our faces.

Lord help us to keep on crying to You for help in our times of trouble.

How many times do I pray for something before I give up?

MON

"Cheer up! On your feet! He's calling you." (Mark 10:49)

Poor Bartimaeus did not have a lot to be happy about. He could not see, which meant he could not work, which in those days meant that he had to beg for his food and money. Worse than this, he would have been looked down on by anyone who passed him by. Although he did not know Jesus, he obviously had heard enough about Him to believe He could help him, so that is why he sat there shouting out His Name. No one thought Jesus would have time to listen to someone like Bartimaeus, but of course He did. We must never be scared to call upon the Name of Jesus ... He will always cheer us up.

Thank You Lord that even though people may look down on us, You never will.

Who do I think looks down on me?

TUES

"I am young in years, and you are old." (Job 32:6)

Age is a strange thing, it can often divide friends and family. When children are young parents spend a lot of time with them and their friends. As they grow older, parents spend less time with them realising that they want to be more with friends of their own age. This is the time that many parents back off too far and lose their close relationship with their children because they consider themselves too old and think that the younger generation would not want to spend time with old people. I think it is very important that young people spend time with their own peer groups, but we older ones must go out of our way to keep close friendships with them.

Lord, thank You for friends of all ages.

Have I got any friends that are not within ten years of my age?

WEDS

It is not only the old who are wise ... who understand what is right.

(Job 32:9)

So often I have heard adults tell children that they must respect their elders. Some think that just because they are older, the younger ones should look up to them. Respect has to be earned by any age. There are some I know, who are older than I am, that I consider totally unwise, even foolish, and I find it hard to respect them. However, there are some much younger than I am who I greatly respect. I would gladly go and get advice from them because I consider them to be wise and I know that they will seek to give me godly instruction that is right. Seek advice from the godly, not just the old.

Lord, thank You for giving wisdom to people younger than ourselves.

What younger people would I go to for godly advice?

THURS

How good and pleasant it is when brothers live together in unity!

(Psa. 133:1)

I have two sons. Now the brothers usually get on very well together and are best friends, but if they have an argument, it seems to take more time to resolve than it would two who are not related. Families seem to set higher standards for each other. I spend my whole life travelling to different church groups and sometimes when I arrive I discover that the church has just split in two because of disagreement. Sometimes these divisions work out for the best, but the sadness comes when neither party is willing to make any compromise to ensure that the separation has at least some Christian values. God wants us to live in unity, and we will need to humble ourselves to see that this happens.

Lord, help us to live in unity with everyone around us.

Who am I not living in unity with?

FRI

Am I now trying to win the approval of men, or of God?

(Gal. 1:10)

Paul continues by saying, "If I were still trying to please men, I would not be a servant of Christ." There have been many times in my life when what people wanted me to do and what God wanted me to do were two different things. Years ago at a youth camp the organisers were arguing with each other and both were trying to get me to support their side. After a couple of days God told me not to get involved so, much to both groups' displeasure, I left them to carry on arguing and I went home. After I had left, the whole camp went down with some sickness bug. I do not ever want to deliberately upset people, but it's more important that I please God than please people.

Lord, help us to do what is right by You.

Do I live to please people or God?

SAT

... you laid the foundations of the earth, and the heavens are the work of your hands. (Psa. 102:25)

I smile as I listen to people trying to convince me of the theory of evolution or some other equally unlikely way that the universe was formed. I am sure they must have a lot more faith than I have to believe some of the incredible things they do. Personally, I have no trouble in believing what the Bible says when it tells me that a Creator God got the whole thing started, and still holds it and us in the palm of His hands. Of course it makes it even easier to believe when the same God who made everything, is also our best friend.

Lord, thank You for creating everything around us that is good.

How do I believe the world began?

SUN

CD 1: 13

For God so loved the world that he gave his one and only Son ...

(John 3:16)

Here is the most famous verse in the Bible and one of the most beautiful. Some people, however, find it difficult to see Father God as loving. Everyone sees Jesus as loving and caring, as He ultimately showed by suffering great agony on a cross because of His love for people. But try and understand how our loving Father God must have felt. He saw the people that He loved and created turn against Him, and realised that the only way that they could be made right was to send to earth His only Son, whom He loved so much, and allow Him to go through such agony. The love of Jesus is wonderful, but so is the love of Father God.

Lord, You gave everything for us, help us give everything for You.

Do I find it easier to understand the love of Jesus, or the love of Father God?

MON

I, Paul, write this greeting in my own hand. (1 Cor. 16:21)

Recently, I was sent an e-mail by a good friend in America whom I have not seen for years. He started off by saying how much he appreciated our friendship and asking how I was keeping, then came his news. Further on he said it would be good to see each other again sometime, and at the end sent greetings from his family. The minute I read that happy memories of his wife and children entered my mind. Many of us are not good at sending greetings unless for a birthday or special occasion. Knowing how much even a note can bless someone, maybe we should regularly send greetings to people at different times of the year.

Lord, help us to regularly make people happy by sending them a greeting.

Who did I last send a greeting to when it was not a special occasion.

TUES

Achan replied, "It is true! I have sinned against the Lord ..." (Josh. 7:20)

If you do not know the sad story of Achan, you must read it. Here was a man who had done something very wrong yet he would not own up and confess. Now you and I do wrong things, but sin cannot be hidden from God, He knows everything. There may come the time when people rightly start accusing us of something that we have done wrong, but we try and deny it. Why deny it? Confess it, apologise, but do not lie about it. If we are punished, then we must live with that deserved punishment but at least our hearts and minds will be in the clear and God will forgive us.

Lord, help us to own up to the wrong that we do.

When did I last not own up to something that I had done wrong?

WEDS

Then all Israel stoned him, and ... the rest ...

(Josh. 7:25)

In the Old Testament some sins were punishable by death and, continuing our story of Achan, his lies and deceit were some of these sins. For us reading this story all these years later, we feel sorry that his family had to suffer and receive the same fate as wicked Achan. I think we all must realise that, even today, when we choose to do wrong things all those around us suffer as well. The sooner we confess our wrongdoing, the sooner we can bring back a bit of happiness into our families.

Lord, help us to realise that when we do wrong, it also affects those who are closest to us.

Can I think of a time when something that I did wrong affected the rest of the family?

THURS

But he replied, "Lord, I am ready to go with you to prison and to death." (Luke 22:33)

Peter was determined to do and say everything that would please Jesus and here he is saying that he is willing to make the ultimate sacrifice for Him. Sadly, a short time after, he denied his friendship with Jesus three times but later, after the resurrection, he did face all sorts of persecution and finally he did die for his best friend, Jesus. We hear amazing stories of Christians in other countries allowing terrible things to happen to them because they refuse to deny their friendship with Jesus. We wonder how we would cope in their situations. We cannot say, but if Jesus really is our best friend, we must not be afraid to stand up for Him at any time.

Lord, help us never to be scared to speak up for You.

How would I cope with persecution?

FRI

God called to him from within the bush, "Moses! Moses!" (Exod. 3:4)

Imagine Moses standing next to a bush that was blazing away, but not burning up; then hearing the voice of God calling his name. Now I am only guessing, but I imagine that God's voice was audible to his ears, in other words, it was a voice booming from somewhere around him and he could not help but hear it. I often wish God spoke to us in that way today, but He usually speaks with that quiet voice into our minds, or through our eyes and hearts as we read the Bible. Mind you, we do have God the Holy Spirit living inside us, so we really have no excuse for not hearing God when He speaks.

Lord, help us to know what Your voice sounds like and to listen when You speak to us.

How does God speak to me?

SAT

And Moses said, "Here I am."

(Exod. 3:4)

Yesterday Moses heard the voice of God, and today he says, "Here I am." Putting the burning bush to one side for a moment, let's imagine if you or I were out by ourselves in a field and we heard someone shout our name. I think I would look around and expect someone to appear who obviously knew me. Moses did not look for a human being, though, somehow he recognised the voice of God and responded. Even today God does sometimes speak using a human voice, in preaching, prophecy and words of knowledge. I wonder if we can discern when it is God or when it is just a human being talking – we need to know the difference.

Lord, help us to know when it's You speaking or when it's a friend just giving advice.

When was I last given the wrong advice?

Week 14

SUN

CD 1: 14

"Do not store up for yourselves treasures on earth ..." (Matt. 6:19)

I love anything new. I was one of the first to get a satellite dish because I saw there were a lot better programmes available. Now I am so busy I rarely have the time or desire to watch TV. I have a big house, which we share with others, and a lovely big garden and I quite enjoy gardening. Now I am so busy I have not really got the time or desire to look after either, the house is starting to fall to bits and the garden is like a jungle. Possessions and "things" are fun, but hardly treasures. The older I get the more I find that these things may be exciting for a short period of time but real treasure can only be found when we are living our lives for Jesus – and that treasure will last forever.

Lord, help us not to live to gain possessions, but to live to please You.

What is my greatest treasure?

MON

"I tell you," he replied, "if they keep quiet, the stones will cry out." (Luke 19:40)

The fever-pitched excitement of the crowd when Jesus entered Jerusalem must have been an amazing thing to see. It's strange that in just a short while probably some of the same crowd would change the word they were shouting from "Hosanna!" to "Crucify!" Jesus is always worthy of our praise and nothing should ever stop us telling Him how much we love Him. I find it strange though how people can change their feelings towards Jesus so quickly. I have met some who have said that they love Jesus, then a short time later they say that they don't even believe in Him. I guess this is the equivalent of shouting "Hosanna" then a short time later shouting "Crucify".

Lord, help us never to say things that would hurt You.

When was the last time I said something that hurt Jesus?

TUES

Sons are a heritage from the Lord, children a reward ... (Psa. 127:3)

It makes me so sad and sometimes, dare I say, angry, when I see and hear adults mistreating children. I watch parents dragging their screaming little one along, shouting and swearing at them as though they were some sort of animal. I see children being ignored in many homes and, worst of all, I see them being treated like inferior beings in church. Children are a reward from God, a special prize in every way. I would not like to be in the shoes of those who abuse God's treasure, on the day when they have to face Him and give account.

Lord, help us to treat children like You do.

How do I treat the children around me?

WEDS

Now there was a man named Joseph, a member of the Council, a good and upright man. (Luke 23:50)

Joseph of Arimathea was a member of the Jewish Sanhedrin, the top religious governing body in the country, which would later be involved in the crucifixion of Jesus. He was surrounded by scribes and Pharisees, many of whom were enemies of Jesus and had no good word to say about Him. Jesus had no good word to say about them either. Nowadays, our advice to Joseph would be to leave them and mix with people who believe what we believe. But Jesus wanted people like Joseph to stay in the Sanhedrin, He wanted His followers to reach all culture groups and the best way to reach people for Jesus is to not ignore those who don't believe, but to spend even more time with them, and befriend them.

Lord, help us to be friends with those who do not yet love You.

Who is my best friend who is not yet a Christian?

THURS

"I will go," she said. (Gen. 24:58)

In Abraham's day their marriage customs were different to today's. Even so, it is great to see God's hand guiding all the way in finding Issac a wife. Do read the story to remind yourself of it. Although some marriages seem to have been arranged, Rebekah was allowed to make up her own mind. She was to meet and marry a man she had never seen, yet she knew it was the right thing to do. This was part of God's plan and when she met her man, they married instantly, and Isaac loved her very much. God will still guide us today regarding our relationships and partners, but only if we let Him and have not already made up our own minds.

Lord, thank You that You want to be involved in our love lives and marriages.

What would I have done if I were Rebekah?

FRI

Stop drinking only water, and use a little wine because of your stomach and your frequent illnesses. (1 Tim. 5:23)

Timothy may have been quite young, but we gather from our reading that he may not have been particularly healthy. It seems quite unusual that Paul should give the above advice. Most of us would have expected him to pray for Timothy, and we would then read that Timothy's stomach problems have been wonderfully and supernaturally healed and he never has those problems again. It seems that while Paul often asked for miracles, at other times he used his common sense and suggested natural healing or pain-relieving remedies. There seems to be definitely a place for both.

Lord, thank You for supernatural healing and also for doctors and medicine.

If ill, who would I go to first, the Lord or a doctor?

SAT

Josiah was eight years old when he became king ... (2 Chron. 34:1)

After a line of really bad kings along comes a good one who would try and bring his kingdom back to worshipping God – eight years old, yet already chosen for a major task in history. However, we must not forget that there must have been older people around him who were giving him godly advice. Children, never forget that God still wants to use you even if you are eight years old or younger but, like Josiah, you will need advice from godly older people around. So adults, keep training up the children, and children, keep expecting to be used by God in wonderful ways!

Lord, help us to believe that you have things for us to do whatever age we are.

How am I a good example to those around me?

SUN

CD 1: 15

On my bed I remember you; I think of you through the watches of the night. (Psa. 63:6)

This is good news for all those who love lying in their beds. King David, that mighty man of action, tells us that as well as thinking of God when he is on the battlefield, he also thinks of Him when he is on his bed. Personally, I don't like lying in bed much, I do not need a lot of sleep and I much prefer to get up and do things as I feel I am wasting my life just lying down. This verse shows me that this is not necessarily so, maybe sometimes I need to stay a little longer in bed because God wants me to just lie there quietly and think about Him.

Lord, help us to think of You as we lie in bed.

Do I spend too much or too little time in my bed?

MON

He poured water into a basin and began to wash his disciples' feet ... (John 13:5)

Where Jesus lived the roads were dusty and people did not wear socks, mostly they wore something like a sandal. This meant their feet would get very dirty. Here Jesus acts like a servant and sees His friends' feet need washing, and sets out to do it for them. Notice that none of the disciples had volunteered to do the task; maybe they felt it was beneath them to get involved with such a menial, smelly act of love. Jesus is the Son of God who loves to serve others, if He serves by washing His friends' feet, how much more should we humble ourselves and serve each other.

Lord, help us to humble ourselves and be willing to serve those around us.

When did I last "serve" someone.

TUES

Keep on loving each other as brothers. (Heb. 13:1)

I was 13 when my little brother Tim was born and at 15 I moved away from home to work on a farm. This meant that I didn't know him very well as he grew up. Later on in life, Tim learned to play the bass guitar and for many years travelled with me as a musician and as a close friend and that friendship is still close today. Sure, we have argued and we have differences of opinion, but our love has always stayed stronger than our disagreement ... because we are brothers. Our verse tells us that we should love all fellow believers around us as part of the family, after all we share the same Heavenly Father so they really are our brothers and sisters.

Lord help us to love the Christians we know like brothers and sisters.

If I have brothers or sisters, do I really love them?

WEDS

Peace be upon Israel. (Psa. 128:6)

The history of Israel has been violent and war seems to follow war, yet this is the nation that God chose to make His own. As Christians we have so much to thank the Jewish people for, even though many have not recognised Jesus as their Messiah and are still waiting for the Messiah to come. Let's pray for Israel as their wars continue, let's pray for peace upon them, but not just peace from attacking armies but, more important, the peace that only Jesus can bring upon those who believe in Him.

Lord, please bring real peace to the people of Israel.

What do I think of Jewish people?

THURS "You will drink from the brook, and I have ordered the ravens to feed you there." (1 Kings 17:4)

Elijah had just spoken the word of the Lord explaining that there would be no rain for the next few years. This would have meant that the drought would make food scarce as well, and I dare say as he ran into hiding he may have been wondering how he was going to survive. God had it all planned, without any supermarket trip to stock up on provisions. Ravens were going to be his waiters. Why do we spend so much time worrying about what food we should buy, it really is no big deal. Elijah did not have a menu, he ate what God gave him. Let's spend more time thinking about Jesus and less time thinking about supermarket lists.

Lord, thank You for giving us food each day.

How would I feel if birds brought me my breakfast each day?

FRI "Son, your sins are forgiven." (Mark 2:5)

Although there are many faiths in the world, what I love about being a Christian is that we believe that Jesus is the Son of God, and we also believe that He has the authority to forgive us when we sin. I try and live a good life, which means that I try not to do, think or say things that would make God sad – but I still sin. It is so good to know that I can go to Jesus and when I am truly sorry for what I have done He not only forgives me, but wipes my sin from His memory.

Lord, thank You that You forgive my sins.

Do I really believe that all my past sins have been forgiven?

SAT

The midwives, however, feared God and did not do what the king ... told them to do. (Exod. 1:17)

The wicked king of Egypt did not want any more Hebrew boys to be born, so he commanded the midwives to destroy the baby boys at birth. The midwives would not do this because they knew this was not what God wanted. In similar ways in some countries going to church, reading the Bible and even believing in Jesus is illegal but Christians know that these laws must be broken and people must be told the good news of Jesus. Today, we must live by laws and rules laid down by governments, but if those laws go against the laws of God, we must be obedient to God not to man.

Lord, help us to live by Your laws.

What would I have done if I had been one of the midwives?

Week 16

SUN

CD 1: 16

"There is no peace," says the Lord, "for the wicked." (Isa. 48:22)

There are people around me who have no time for Jesus and no desire to live the way that He would like them to live. So why are they better off than I am? They have great big houses, brand new cars, holidays in the Bahamas every year and more money in the bank than I could earn in a lifetime. Am I jealous? Well, maybe, sometimes after all they do seem to have everything – but have they? The Bible tells us that the one thing they cannot buy is peace. Real peace is better than all the money in the world and it is only given to those who love Jesus.

Lord, we may not be rich, but we can live in peace.

Am I jealous of anyone?

MON

Without faith it is impossible to please God ... (Heb. 11:6)

Faith is simply believing in things that have not yet happened, and things we cannot see. When we pray for someone who is ill and we want to see God heal them, we have to ask Him to give us faith to believe that they will be made well again and even to give us "eyes" that can imagine and see them back to full health. The Christian life is full of faith. We needed faith to put our trust in the Lord Jesus when we first became Christians as we could not see Him with our eyes even though we believed that He is real and alive. Let's keep asking God for more faith.

Lord, we want to live to please You, please give us more faith.

How much faith have I really got?

TUES

"If any one of you is without sin, let him be the first to throw a stone at her." (John 8:7)

Here was a woman caught in the act of doing something that was very wrong and the religious leaders were saying that she deserved the death penalty for her sin. Jesus wrote something on the ground; we do not know what it was but the accusers read it and then Jesus challenged them with today's Scripture verse. It's so easy to think of big sins and little sins, very wicked sinners as opposed to nice people who sometimes sin. Sin is sin and we should never be judging others when we ourselves are also sinners.

Lord, help us not to condemn others.

What do I think that Jesus wrote on the ground?

WEDS "Go now and leave your life of sin." (John 8:11)

Yesterday's scripture was about the woman who had sinned and her accusers who, when challenged by Jesus, all went away realising that they too were sinners. Now Jesus faces this woman. He does not just say be thankful and go back and enjoy your life. He tells her to go, but also that she must now stop doing the wrong things that she had been doing. Jesus forgives us, but He is not pleased if once we have been forgiven we keep going back and carrying on doing the same old sins again and again.

Lord, please help us to stop doing the things that make You sad.

What sin do I still carry on doing regularly?

THURS The Lord watches over all who love him ... (Psa. 145:20)

Often I find I am alone and facing a difficult situation or decision. Irene's not around, nor are my friends that I would normally seek advice from. It's at times like these when I remember today's reading, I may feel alone but I am not alone. The Lord is with me and watching me. I try not to rush into just a rational or logical answer, I try and find a bit of space to ask the Lord what I should do. Jesus is always with us as our constant friend and companion.

Lord, thank You for watching over us.

Where can I go to find a bit of space to be with the Lord?

FRI

May your blessing be on your people. (Psa. 3:8)

The Lord is so generous, He enjoys giving good things to those who love Him, serve Him and ask for their needs to be met. Yes, asking is important. When my children want something they do not wait until I guess what they would like, they come up to me and make their request known. Sometimes I may say no for various reasons, but more often than not I say yes because I enjoy giving them things they like. How much more does our Heavenly Father want to give us His children good things, but let's remember to ask politely and not be disappointed if for some reason He says no.

Lord, please bless us today.

What would I like to receive from Heavenly Father today?

SAT

Nobody should seek his own good, but the good of others. (1 Cor. 10:24)

The Christian life is wonderful, there is so much we can do, and so much fun we can have, in fact we can do anything except those things that the Bible lays down as sin. Sin breaks our relationship with God. Now, although we can do so many things, we do have to be thoughtful of others. We are not living just to please ourselves, we are living to please God and He always reminds us to think of those around and be sure that what we are doing is not being unhelpful to them or might make them fall.

Lord, help us not to do things that might cause others to fall.

Have I ever done anything that may cause others to fall?

SUN

CD 1: 17

For the Lamb at the centre of the throne will be their shepherd.

(Rev. 7:17)

In my days working on the farm I met many old shepherds. These men would do anything for their sheep even if it meant staying out all night to look after them in lambing season. I often thought that these shepherds thought more of their sheep than their families, but then realised that for some of them the sheep were included as part of their families. I have also seen many tiny lambs being born. They look weak, frail and helpless. The Lamb of God is a name given to Jesus, but the Lamb of God is not weak, He is all-powerful. Jesus the Lamb is also Jesus the Good Shepherd and He at this very moment is sitting on a throne in heaven, watching over and caring for you and me.

Lord, thank You for being both the Lamb of God and the Good Shepherd.

What do I think Jesus is doing at this very minute?

MON

"Get up and eat, for the journey is too much for you." (1 Kings 19 v 7)

Elijah had been running everywhere and doing some amazing things for God, but now he was hungry and tired. I guess God could have given him extra strength supernaturally so he could have carried on without resting and eating but instead the angel of the Lord told him that his body needed food and drink. Nowadays we see God do impossible and supernatural things, but often He tells us to use the natural and just be sensible. We need to be willing to do the natural but also be open for God to perform the supernatural.

Lord, help us to take care of our bodies.

What was the last supernatural thing that I saw God do?

TUES

On the first day of the week we came together to break bread.

(Acts 20:7)

It will always be a mystery how Sunday became a special day for Christians. We know that up until the book of Acts, the Jews had always considered the last day in the week (the Sabbath) to be the special day, but now we see that some of the Christians had changed it to the first day – from the Saturday to the Sunday. Sunday in those days was a normal working day so the Christians would have had to have their meetings before and after work. Nowadays, although most Christians prefer to meet together on Sundays, I believe that every day is special, so let's worship Jesus seven days a week not just on Sundays.

“” **Lord thank You for seven special days each week.**

? **What day do I consider to be most special?**

WEDS

But Moses said, “Oh Lord, please send someone else to do it.”

(Exod. 4:13)

It's easy for us to look at Moses and consider him a bit of a coward. He had heard from God, God promised to be with him and still he wanted to pull out and God to send someone else. As we read on we can see the mighty task he was facing with both Pharaoh and the children of Israel. Before we condemn Moses, think: How do we cope when God wants us to go and tell someone who is not yet a Christian about Jesus, when maybe that someone is a person we don't know or, worse still, a relative? Have you ever thought, Lord please send someone else to do it? I think we all have at one time or another.

“” **Lord, help us to be willing to do all You ask.**

? **When was the last time that I was scared to do something?**

THURS

If anyone does not know how to manage his own family, how can he take care of God's church? (1 Tim. 3:5)

In my teenage years, I was far from God and living a life of rebellion. My godly father resigned from church leadership because of this scripture. Was he right in doing so? Well I cannot question what he felt he should do, but I would like to add this. Discipline in the home is very important, if we cannot lead our families of course we have no right to lead a "flock". However, when a child becomes an adult, I don't think this scripture applies. Once adult, our children are answerable directly to God, not to us parents. That is why it is so important to train up our children in the ways of God, while they are young.

Lord, help us to be good leaders to all those around.

At what age do I think that a child becomes an adult?

FRI

Sing to the Lord a new song. (Psa. 149:1)

I spend a lot of my time enjoying listening to recordings that people send me of new songs they have written. In my opinion there is no such thing as a bad song, because the writers have put the words and tunes together as an expression of their heart and how they feel. Sometimes I hear a new song that touches my heart as I listen to it. I think we should all be able to put a few words together and add a little tune and sing a new song to the Lord, it really is a very easy thing to do.

Lord, please put a new song in our hearts today.

Can I make up a little praise song now?

SAT

If you are insulted because of the name of Christ, you are blessed.

(1 Pet. 4:14)

Sometimes we are frightened to tell our friends about Jesus or to admit we are Christians and belong to a church because we are scared of the reaction we might get. Those we tell may make fun of us or, worse still, tell all their friends about us so a lot of people make fun of us. Our reading today tells us not to worry about what people think of us or say to us. If we speak out about Jesus when He wants us to, we will be blessed by God, and that is more precious than any nasty things that people can say about us.

Lord, help us not to worry if people make fun of us because we are Your followers.

When was the last time someone said something horrible to me?

Week 18

SUN

CD 1: 18

"This, then, is how you should pray ..."

(Matt. 6:9–13)

Here we have the most wonderful prayer in the Bible, the one that the Lord Jesus taught His disciples to pray and the one that we should all be able to remember and pray as well. Notice how short and to the point it is. I pray with many children and adults and usually I much prefer to listen to children's prayers. Adults tend to use a lot of words and take ages to say what they want to say, and instead of naturally "chatting to God" they sometimes end up giving Him a sermon. Children's prayers are much more real and natural. Their prayer consists of just a few words to their best friend Jesus, who they know is not only listening to them, but also is interested in what they are saying.

Lord, teach us to pray, in a real way.

Do I prefer prayer meetings or just praying by myself?

MON

Altogether, Methuselah lived 969 years, and then he died. (Gen. 5:27)

Now this is a long life. In his 500s he would have been regarded as middle-aged and he was still fathering children. He would have seen a lot of changes. Today, some people reach 100, yet they would have seen more changes in the last 80 years than Methuselah did in his 969 years. Look at our transport, rockets, medicine, communication; we have advanced a long way in a very short time but it's sad that mankind personally has not advanced. Man is still selfish, unforgiving, cruel and spiritually lost. People desperately need to get to know Jesus who can bring about the greatest change of all. I wonder how many more years that will take?

“” **Lord, we pray that others will want to know You as they see the changes You have made in our lives.**

? **What is the greatest change that I have seen in my life?**

TUES

Their mind is on earthly things. (Phil. 3:19)

During my holiday I took time out to read through Isaiah and Jeremiah which I must confess are not books I usually rush to read. Time and time again God's prophets were telling people that it was wrong to have gods of iron, wood and stone. It suddenly occurred to me that we are not so different today. How easy it is for us Christians to make idols of our cars and houses, still "things" made out of iron, wood and stone. We must try and get our minds off these earthly "things" and concentrate on Jesus and living for the kingdom of God.

“” **Lord, we pray that earthly "things" never become more important to us than You.**

? **Do I own anything that is more important to me than God is?**

WEDS

Praise him with the clash of cymbals ... (Psa. 150:5)

Imagine walking into a church meeting and noticing that the musician about to lead us at the front is not sitting at a keyboard or playing a guitar – the main musician is holding two massive cymbals that at some stage during our praise time are going to be clashed together. Some would complain before the first clash sounded. Our cymbal player is of course perfectly biblical. We must learn to appreciate all different styles of instruments and praise music and not just be always wanting the style and instruments that suit us.

Thank You Lord for all types of percussion and musical instruments.

What instrument would I most like to be able to play well?

THURS

Jesus said to them, "Come and have breakfast." (John 21:12)

Jesus had risen again from the dead and was still performing miracles. This time He was helping out His weary fishing friends who seemed to have lost the knack of catching fish! He had the fire prepared and told them to bring some fish over to cook for breakfast. Jesus was not just interested in preaching to people, He was interested in giving them what they needed and He knew a breakfast would cheer these boys up. Let us today show love to people and do things for them that will make them happy.

Lord, give us an opportunity to show Your love today to someone in a practical way.

How do I show love to people?

FRI

"Who touched me?" Jesus asked.

(Luke 8:45)

I can imagine why Peter thought this a strange thing for Jesus to ask, after all, they were surrounded by a crowd who would have been pushing and pressing against Him from all sides. Jesus knew someone was in need of His power and had touched Him to receive it. This must have required great faith from the woman concerned who was ill, and it is not surprising that she was healed. Today we cannot physically touch Jesus, but we can touch Him in our prayers and it's good to know that He still has the same power to heal and help those who believe.

Lord, when we need healing help us to reach out in faith and touch You.

What is the worst crowd that I have been caught up in?

SAT

Then Samuel said, "Speak, for your servant is listening." (1 Sam. 3:10)

I often wish God would always speak to me in visions and dreams. I find it easier to believe that it is God saying something when I wake up remembering a vivid dream I have just had. The Lord is our Father, and just like any good father He always has things to say to His children. I wonder how many times each day the Lord calls us by name, but we ignore Him, thinking it is just our mind playing games with us. Let's not risk missing out. Even if we only think it could be God's voice, let's say, "Speak Lord your servant is listening ... " we could be surprised by what follows!

Lord, please speak to us today, Your servants are listening.

How can I be sure that it is God speaking to me?

SUN

CD 1: 19

"Be strong and be courageous ..." (Deut. 31:7)

I used to smile as we sang the well-known song "Be bold, be strong" which includes the line "I am not afraid, no no no", because I knew there were people around me singing away who were afraid of the dark, spiders and definitely dogs! I know children who are afraid to say no when their school friends encourage them to do wrong things, and parents who are even scared to discipline their children. If we are singing that we are not afraid of the evil one, surely we need to ask God to help us not to be scared by other fears. We need to be strong and courageous in the whole of life, not just in spiritual warfare.

Lord, help us to be really strong and courageous.

What am I frightened of?

MON

Now if we are children, then we are heirs ... (Rom. 8:17)

If we think we are poor this verse should cheer us up as it reminds us that as well as being children of God we are also His heirs and He has more riches than we could ever imagine to pass on to us. There is one snag, however, as heirs we will also share in His suffering in order that we might share in His glory. In other words we can expect hard and difficult times on this earth when we are followers of Jesus but we have great things to look forward to. It's worth hanging on in there, even though at times we may feel like giving up. As His children we must also realise that our Father is here to help us, every step of the way.

Lord, it's an honour to be an heir of Yours.

When did I last feel like giving up on something?

TUES

Moses threw [his staff] on the ground and it became a snake, and he ran from it. (Exod. 4:3)

Moses at this time has a lot to learn about the power of God. He understandably thinks he will fail if he has to stand in front of the king of Egypt so God tells him to throw his walking stick onto the floor and suddenly it changes into a snake and starts wriggling around in front of him. It makes Moses jump and he runs away from it. We must realise that God is all-powerful and when He asks us to do something He will give us everything we need to help us complete the task successfully.

Lord, thank You for providing us with all we need to fulfil Your plans

Are there any creatures that I do not like?

WEDS

The Lord said to him, "Reach out your hand and take it by the tail." (Exod. 4:4)

Yesterday we realised that snakes were not Moses' favourite creatures, in fact he was clearly scared of them. His walking stick is now slithering about in front of him and God tells him to grab the snake's tail. I think most of us would have found this hard to do, but when he did it, the snake changed back into a stiff wooden pole. There are things that God may tell us to do that look both stupid and dangerous, but if God says do something, He will also take the danger out of the situation and show us He is Lord of absolutely everything. Even snakes.

Lord, help us not to live in fear of any of the creatures that You have created.

Would I have dared to grab the snake's tail?

THURS He calls his own sheep by name ... (John 10:3)

Jesus is not just the Good Shepherd, He is the very best shepherd that has ever existed. We Christians are likened to the sheep that He looks after. Just think, since the beginning of time I wonder how many people have truly loved God? We are talking about a massive amount of people. Now consider how many people are following Jesus throughout the whole world today, again a mega number. Isn't it great to know that even with such a huge amount of sheep to look after, Jesus still knows us individually by name and is our own personal friend.

Lord, thank You that You not only know our names, You know all about us.

Which country do I think has the least number of Christians living in it?

FRI Do not rebuke an older man harshly, but exhort him as if he were your father. (1 Tim. 5:1)

Respecting our elders is quite biblical, but we do need to realise that even older men sometimes do and say wrong things and need to be challenged on them. Paul advises that correction is brought gently, but it still must be brought; everyone, whatever their age, needs to be accountable and teachable. Today the same thing must happen, the only problem is many younger leaders are scared to challenge senior people who may have been believers for much longer than they have, and some of our seniors may have become a little proud and will not take discipline from those younger than themselves. Both of the above need to change if we want church to be as Jesus wants it to be.

Lord, help us all to be willing to receive godly correction from each other.

Would I be scared to bring correction to an older person?

SAT

Do not forget to entertain strangers ... some have entertained angels without knowing it. (Heb. 13:2)

It's very easy to become people of set routine and mark out days when we need our space and privacy and be so rigid that we refuse to let anything change this. I believe we should always remain flexible and although having plans is not wrong, we must always be willing to change them if God wants us to. Imagine we have just settled in for the night with a nice meal and a film to watch and the doorbell rings. We must answer it because it may be someone God has sent round for us to entertain or, even more important, it may just happen to be a passing angel and no cosy night in could be anywhere near as exciting as entertaining one of God's messengers could it?

Lord, help us to be people who enjoy entertaining others.

Did I enjoy the last time I entertained someone?

Week 20

SUN

CD 1: 20

Do not let your mouth lead you into sin. (Eccl. 5:6)

Since my dad died, I try and visit my mum every Monday which is always a lot of fun. Sometimes we do a bit of gardening, other times we go to the local garden centre café and have coffee and a bacon sandwich, but whatever we do, we do a lot of talking. We talk about our churches, we debate together over certain scriptures and we always update each other on how our mutual friends and relations are doing. There is nothing wrong with this, but we must be careful. What we are saying could be a harmless update of news, but this can easily lead to gossip and then become sin. We must all be very careful with what we say and we must think before we speak, and try and stop our mouths leading us into sin.

Lord, help us not to say the wrong things.

When did I last "gossip" about someone?

MON

In the beginning God created the heavens and the earth. (Gen. 1:1)

Some people have the weirdest ideas of how the heavens and the earth began. Some would say there was a great big bang – and earth was there. But who caused the big bang? Others would say we all evolved from the tiniest creature imaginable – but who made the first tiniest creature imaginable? At the end of the day the Bible is the only sensible explanation. In the beginning God created – Still, the question will be asked, Who made God? but what makes God, God, is that He could not have been made – He has always been – and always will be!

Lord, thank You for creating all things.

What do I think of the evolution theory?

TUES

So the soldiers took the money and did as they were instructed. (Matt. 28:15)

The body of Jesus had gone from the tomb, the resurrection had happened and Jesus had come back to life again. The Jewish religious leaders did not want this news to get out, so they bribed the soldiers who were guarding the tomb and told them to tell everyone that while they slept, the disciples came and stole the body of Jesus. What a crazy thing to say. How would they know who stole the body if they were asleep? Some people today still do not want to believe that Jesus is alive and loves talking to His friends. You and I know the Bible tells the true story, so let's never give up telling them the truth of what really happened to Jesus.

Lord, thank You for being alive today.

What proof do I have that Jesus is alive today?

WEDS He won over the hearts of all the men of Judah ... (2 Sam. 19:14)

King David had many difficult times during his reign and he by no means always made the right decisions. David's great strength, however, was that he could draw people around him and, without manipulation or pressure, could win their hearts and get them on his side. So often both in the home and in church life decisions are made by parents and leaders and both children and congregations are expected to agree without ever being won over. Both parents and church leaders should learn from David how to win the hearts of their listeners and then they will find people agree with them because they choose to, not because they are expected to.

Lord, show us how to win the hearts of people.

How would I win over the heart of someone?

THURS When he was sound asleep, he fell to the ground from the third storey ... (Acts 20:9)

Paul was preaching a rather long sermon, and it was now midnight. A young man called Eutychus who was sitting on a window ledge, dozed off and fell out of the window falling three storeys to the ground below. Everyone rushed outside and saw he was dead, but Paul threw his arms around him and a miracle happened, to everyone's relief he came back to life again. Paul then continued the meeting until daylight. People were hungry to learn about God. Let's not moan about the length of time people preach for, let's listen and learn from our Bible teachers and praise God for them. Even having a sleep is better than complaining, but I do not suggest you sit on a window ledge!

Lord, thank You for those who teach us more about the truths from the Bible.

Have I ever fallen asleep in a church meeting?

FRI

Timothy, my fellow-worker, sends his greetings to you ... (Rom. 16:21)

At the end of a letter, it's always nice to hear that other friends and family who had not written the letter pass on their love, best wishes or greetings. In this letter to the Romans not just Timothy but a few other names are added to the list sending greetings. When I send letters and e-mails I often add, "Irene and the family send their love", but do they? Sometimes they never even hear about the communication I have had, because I forget to tell them. I think we must be honest in all we say and do. I am sure most of the time Irene and the family would want me to send on their greetings, but it's right that I ask them first – and not just make things up.

Lord, help us to be honest, even in the little things, like sending greetings.

Do I ever add words onto letters that are not strictly true?

SAT

Teach me what I cannot see ... (Job 34:32)

The scripture continues, "if I have done wrong, I will not do so again". Most of the time we know when we have done wrong things, someone either tells us, or we feel bad inside. Sometimes, however, we just cannot see that we have done wrong and instead of asking God to show us if we have unknowingly slipped up, we spend all our time arguing that we are in the right. I want to be open to be shown all the wrong I do, so hopefully I will learn my lessons and stop doing things that I should not do.

Lord, please help us to face up to all wrong things that we do.

Do I like to argue that I am right, even if I know I am wrong?

SUN

CD 1: 21

But God demonstrates his own love for us in this: While we were still sinners, Christ died for us. (Rom 5:8)

I always have and always will love my children, but when they have done something wrong and I have had to punish them, they may not feel that I do. They may wrongly feel that I love them more when they are being good. God's love for us never changes. When we were at our worst and had no good in us, God showed just how much He loved us by allowing his only Son, Jesus, to come down to earth to give us the chance to be made clean inside and right with Him. That love for us is always there.

Lord, thank You that whatever we do, You never stop loving us.

Do I feel that people love me more when I am good than when I am bad?

MON

He said to them, "Watch out! Be on your guard against all kinds of greed ... " (Luke 12:15a)

Some people think that greed is just eating more food than we need. The dictionary, however, also says greed is excessive desire for wealth and power. We can experience greed, for example, when we meet someone who has something that we would like to have, and we then desperately want it for ourselves. For children this could be another child's toy, for adults it could be a house, a car or even a holiday. Jesus is very kind and generous but He does not like us to be greedy in any way.

Lord, please help us not to be greedy.

When was the last time that I was greedy?

TUES

"A man's life does not consist in the abundance of his possessions."

(Luke 12:15b)

Yesterday we looked at greed, today we are looking at the second half of the verse. I have so many possessions and sometimes wonder why I have them all. I do not need most of them, and they certainly do not help me get closer to being like Jesus. Last week I filled up many rubbish bags with "things" and got rid of them. It was not easy though, because as I put some of these possessions in the bags, a little voice kept telling me to hang onto them. I believe that the less possessions I have, the more I will be like my friend Jesus so, be quiet little voice and let's make another trip to the rubbish tip.

Lord, help us not to collect worthless possessions here on earth.

What possession would I find most hard to part with?

WEDS

Our mouths were filled with laughter ... (Psa. 126:2a)

Good things had happened to the people of Israel and this caused their mouths to be full of laughter. It's funny but I find that the same thing often happens to me. At the end of a "Praise Party" I sometimes meet up with friends and find I am so excited about what I have just been involved in that I cannot seem to stop myself laughing. It can even be a bit embarrassing for them sometimes! I do not need someone to tell a joke or tickle me I just find it comes as a natural expression of the way I am feeling. Laughter is a wonderful relaxing gift from God and I thank Him for it.

Lord, thank You that we can laugh.

What makes me laugh?

THURS ... our tongues with songs of joy.

(Psa. 126:2b)

Yesterday we saw how the Israelites were filled with laughter, today we can see that the laughter led to songs of joy. Again, I find I often have a similar experience. God does so many wonderful things in my life that often I burst into singing songs of joy to Him. Now although I have made many albums, I am the first to admit that I do not have the voice of a songbird, but that will never stop me singing my praises to God, although sometimes I do sing quietly if there are a lot of people around. Come on everyone, it does not matter if we are good singers or not, let's sing songs of joy to the Lord!

Lord, help us never to be frightened to sing songs of joy to You.

If I burst into a song of praise, which song would I sing?

FRI ... whoever believes in him shall not perish but have eternal life.

(John 3:16)

The second half of the most famous verse in the Bible is so exciting for us. To "believe in Jesus" does not just mean to believe that He existed 2,000 years ago and walked around Israel just doing good things. To believe means to believe that Jesus is God's Son who came to earth, did no wrong but ended up being crucified so we sinners could be made right with Father God. It also means believing that He rose again from the dead and is alive today. If we truly believe this, we are promised that although our bodies may die, we will never perish – we will live for ever and ever with Jesus – Wow !

Lord, thank You that if we believe in Jesus, we are going to live forever.

What parts of Jesus' life on earth do I find it hardest to believe?

SAT

The Lord said to Moses, "Why are you crying out to me?" (Exod. 14:15)

Moses had led the Israelites out of Egypt and now their route was blocked by a massive sea. He told the people to stand still, while God told them to move on. God is guiding us all through life, and so often when we face a huge problem blocking our way forward like Moses we feel the right thing to do is to stop, pray about it and wait for God to remove the object. I believe that often God says to us what He said to Moses: I have already told you where I want you to go, just keep walking and as you continue, I will remove the problems, or part the sea. Let's not just stand around, let's get on with fulfilling our calling, for time is short.

Lord, help us not to stand still instead of moving on.

Have I any problems that may be blocking me from moving on with God?

Week 22

SUN

CD 1: 22

There are different kinds of gifts, but the same Spirit. (1 Cor. 12:4)

In 1 Corinthians 12:8–10 we have a list which Christians usually refer to as the "gifts of the Holy Spirit". These are supernatural presents that God gives to those who both want them and need them. The great news is that He does not just give them to adults. Many times I have heard children praising God in tongues and seen young ones praying for people who are not well and seeing them healed. These gifts do not make us more spiritual, but they do show those around us that Jesus is alive and as powerful as He ever has been.

Lord, thank You for all Your supernatural gifts.

What "gifts of the Holy Spirit" have I used?

MON

But the fruit of the Spirit is love ... (Gal. 5:22)

But not just love. It's also joy, peace, patience, kindness, goodness, faithfulness, gentleness and self-control. Try and imagine that we are like fruit trees. When we first became a Christian our branches were very bare but the more we get to be like Jesus the more His wonderful fruit mentioned above begins to both grow and show in our lives. Some Christians become very impatient because the fruit takes a while to show. Fruit always takes time to grow, and some fruit takes longer than others, but one thing is guaranteed, the closer we walk with Jesus, the nicer people we will be.

Lord, help us to show the fruit of the Spirit in our lives.

What "fruit of the Spirit" seems to take the longest time to grow in my life?

TUES

Elijah ... bent down to the ground and put his face between his knees. (1 Kings 18:42)

Elijah had prophesied that there would be no rain for years. After that time has passed, Elijah tells the king there will now be rain. Then he climbs up to the top of Mount Carmel to pray and we suddenly find him in this strange prayer position – bending down to the ground with his face between his knees. People pray in many different positions. Some kneel, some sit or stand, I sometimes like lying flat on the floor and at other times walking about. The position we choose to pray in is not important, keeping our mind on Jesus is.

Lord, whatever position we choose to pray in, help us to think of You.

What position do I most like to pray in?

WEDS

The servant reported, "A cloud as small as a man's hand is rising."

(1 Kings 18:44)

Elijah remained in his praying position, not looking up to the sky for signs of rain but looking up to God for His prayer to be answered. His servant was on the look-out. After his first look, the servant said there was no sign of rain but Elijah told him to go back and keep looking. It was going to take seven trips. After the seventh, he saw the tiny cloud come out of the sea, God had answered Elijah's prayer, the rain was coming. Sometimes God answers our prayers immediately, sometimes He does not. Like Elijah, let's not ever give up praying because God will answer our prayer in His time not ours.

Lord, help us to keep our eyes on You because You always answer our prayers.

Would I rather be Elijah or his servant?

THURS

"Sir," the invalid replied, "I have no-one to help me ..." (John 5:7)

This poor man who had been an invalid for 38 years was lying by the so-called healing pool of Bethesda waiting for someone to help him into the water when it stirred. But everyone was too busy looking after themselves to help this unfortunate person. Then Jesus appeared and, making no mention of the water, He healed him on the spot. It is very easy for us to just think of ourselves, when all around us are people saying, "I have no one to help me." Let's make time for those that really need our help even if it means changing our plans and putting ourselves out.

Lord, help us to care for those who need our help

Do I think that the water in the pool could really heal someone?

FRI

The Lord answered, "Listen to them and give them a king." (1 Sam. 8:22)

God did not want Israel to be like all the other nations around and have a human king to rule them. He was there to lead and guide them. The people, however, kept on telling Samuel that they needed a king, and in the end God had to, sadly, give in to them and let them have one. God has given people the freedom to choose and He will never take that away from us. Still today we sometimes choose to put people in God's place. We look to church leaders and those with prophetic ministries to lead and guide us. Although we respect and listen to these people, God is our King and He is the One we should be listening to for our instructions for living.

Lord, You are our King and the One who will guide us.

Who would I go to for advice first, God or a friend?

SAT

John wore clothing made of camel's hair, with a leather belt round his waist ... (Mark 1:6)

Keeping up with the latest fashion and wearing all the trendy designer clothes was never a godly or biblical thing to do. Here we have probably the least trendy non-fashion victim in the Bible, John the Baptist. Even by his day's standards he was dressed rather strangely and very few people would have said, "I want to look like John". And yet here was a man who was so close to God. The style of clothes we wear is not important, and we should never make a big deal about them. It's not what we wear on the outside that's significant, it's what is happening inside our lives that is important.

Lord, help us not to spend too much time thinking about clothes and fashion.

What clothes do I think I look best in?

SUN

CD 1: 23

The fear of the Lord is the beginning of wisdom ... (Prov. 9:10)

People in Bible times repeatedly saw how powerful God was, and only fools did not fear Him. Even the most holy were frightened to be in His presence. The fear of the Lord is mentioned 14 times in Proverbs but it does not just mean that we should be frightened of God, it also means we should have a very deep reverence and respect for Him. Do we live in fear of the Lord? Most people today do not, in fact many make fun of Him, while others say that He does not exist. These people are not wise and one day, unless they change, I am afraid they will discover how foolish they have been and then they will be very frightened by who He is and by what He can do.

Lord, You are God and we do fear You, but You are also our Father and we love You.

Who do I know who makes fun of God?

MON

Whoever loves money never has money enough. (Eccl. 5:10)

Very few people would say that they do not like having money. Most of us would like enough to live comfortably and not have to worry about getting into debt. But the truth still remains, the more money we have the more money we want and this is the same for children, young people and adults. Every day we read about multi-millionaires who do not need any more money and if they lived to be a thousand they could never spend all they have, yet they still need more. Having money is not wrong, but loving it and living for it is, and those people that live in this way will never be satisfied. Let's learn to be satisfied with what we have.

Lord, thank You for money, help us to be satisfied with what we have.

Have I got enough money?

TUES

"The fathers have eaten sour grapes, and the children's teeth are set on edge." (Jer. 31:29)

Here was a popular proverb of the day meaning that a person's sins can affect his family. The people of Jeremiah's time felt that God was angry with them, not because they had done anything wrong, but because of the sins of those who went before them. We know that the way parents behave can affect their children, but we also know that God judges each person for the good and bad they do, and He will never blame children for their parents' wrongdoing. So, young ones, you cannot always blame the older ones, but older ones, we must be very careful what we do and say in front of children because we can be passing an example onto them that is not good.

Lord, help us to see that often we are responsible for the things we do wrong and we can't always blame others.

When did I last blame someone else?

WEDS

Make every effort to live in peace with all men ... (Heb. 12:14)

I have quite a few faults, as those close to me know. One of them is that if I see an argument or debate, I love to join in. Mind you I do not like it if it gets "heated" and people start to lose their tempers or get hurt. I think certain things are worth discussing, but getting angry with each other over points of disagreement can never be right. I will probably never stop being involved in debates but I must learn that certain subjects are not worth arguing about. We all have different viewpoints, but to live in peace and love and friendship is more important than to win any argument.

Lord, help us to live in peace with those we disagree with.

Do I enjoy arguing?

THURS

For you were once darkness, but now you are light in the Lord.

(Eph. 5:8)

I love the sun and the summer when the daytime seems to last forever and the darkness of the night is very short. Waking up and getting up in the morning is never a problem when the sun shines through the window. However, as the seasons change there seems to be more darkness than light. We Christians are no longer depressing darkness, we are bright and warm and should make those around us feel good. Jesus is the light of the world, let's make sure that His light shines out in us today.

Lord help us to be like bright warm light to those around us.

Do people see me as a happy or rather miserable person?

FRI

Jesus said, "Whoever has my commands and obeys them, he is the one who loves me." (John 14:21)

I often asked my children to tidy their bedrooms or to put their toys away, but for one reason or another they did not do it and Irene and I had to. My children would always say that they loved me, but I would tell them that if they really loved me, they would show it by doing what I asked them to do. Being obedient to Jesus is even more important. Many people say that they love Jesus, but when He asks them to do something they don't do it. Jesus tells us that the only way to prove that we really do love Him is to do whatever He asks, this should not be so hard as we all know that Jesus only wants the very best for us.

Lord, we do love You, help us to show it.

How do I show that I love my family?

SAT

The whole assembly bowed in worship, while the singers sang and the trumpeters played. (2 Chron. 29:28)

King Hezekiah wanted to worship and give thanks to the Lord. He also wanted to praise God with music and singing. Out came the musicians with their cymbals, harps, lyres (a stringed instrument, not someone who tells untruths!) and trumpets. They were going to make a lot of noise as they praised. As they sang everyone bowed in the presence of God to worship Him. Sometimes at our meetings we sing a lot of great songs and hear wonderful musicians, but do not really worship God. Let's remember that the main reason we gather together as a church is to worship God not just enjoy music.

“” **Lord, when we are praising You, help us to think of You and not just the music that we are enjoying.**

? **Does music help me to praise God, or is it a distraction?**

Week 24

SUN

CD 1: 24

"The harvest is plentiful but the workers are few." (Matt. 9:37)

The farming calender follows a similar pattern each year. During the autumn, winter and spring there is always plenty of work to do, but there also seems to be plenty of time to do it. Then comes the summer and the corn is ripe and ready to harvest. Until the corn is safely inside the barn, there is little rest for the workers. When I was on the farm, we would work from dawn till dark because we knew that we only had a limited time to harvest the fields. Jesus tells us that today time is also limited and that people around us need to hear about His love. He says that the harvest is ready, but the workers are few. We are workers for Jesus, let's help get the harvest in.

“” **Lord, help us to work hard to help get Your harvest in.**

? **What is my busiest time of the year?**

MON

Jesus spoke all these things to the crowd in parables. (Matt. 13:34)

Jesus often spoke to the crowds using little short stories that had meanings much deeper than the obvious. This meant that all the listeners had to listen very carefully to the story that Jesus told, because it was not written down. Then they had to work out what Jesus was trying to teach them. Sadly, nowadays we very rarely are taught by stories, and if we are, we are told the meaning rather than having to think it through for ourselves. Television and computer games give our brain very little to think about. God gave each of us a good brain, let's use it.

Lord, thank You that You gave us a brain so we can think things through.

What stimulates my brain?

TUES

Why, O Lord, do you stand far off? (Psa. 10:1)

In the Old Testament, when things went wrong the Jews felt that God was far away from them and that was the reason why He did not rush to help them. The great news for us is that since the day of Pentecost we know that God will never be far away from the Christian because when we give our lives to Jesus, God the Holy Spirit comes and lives within us. God can't ever be closer to us than that!

Lord, thank You for living in each of us.

What signs are there that the Holy Spirit is living within me?

WEDS

And now, dear children, continue in him ... (1 John 2:28)

My son, Joss, and I decided to go out and play a round of golf. As we prepared to hit that little white ball off the first tee, we felt rather nervous, but very excited. We hoped that this was going to be our best round yet. By hole 12 Joss was having a terrible game and told me he was going to pack it in as it was no fun. I persuaded him to carry on and actually he picked up and started playing well. I have met many who start following Jesus and are very excited about it, but after a while when times are difficult they want to pack it in. We Christians will have hard times, but we must continue to follow Jesus and never give up.

Lord, help us to always follow You.

Should I ever give up when playing a game?

THURS

Now Jericho was tightly shut up because of the Israelites. (Josh. 6:1)

Here was this massive fortress called Jericho which the newly-formed Israelite army had no hope of conquering without the help of God. The people of Jericho had the gates tightly shut, no one was allowed in and no one was allowed out. They felt very safe. Sometimes when we sit in our houses with all the doors and windows locked and with our security alarms on we think we are very safe. Safety does not come just by being protected by strong walls, but we can find real safety in the most dangerous of places when we obey Jesus and stay close to Him.

Lord, help us to remember that walls do not protect us, You do.

When do I most feel safe?

FRI

Do not say, "Why were the old days better than these?" (Eccl. 7:10)

I love thinking back to the "good old days". I believe the best era for music was the 1960s and that's the music I enjoy listening to on my many long car journeys. Why does the past always seem so rosy? I think most of the time our memories only choose to remember the things we enjoyed, and the times when things went well. If we thought about the past for a bit longer we might also recollect the sad times, the bad times and the times when things went wrong. Let's not be fooled, the old days were no better than today, today is much more exciting, God has new plans for us, let's get on and live for now.

Lord, we can remember the past, but help us not to live in it.

What is my best memory?

SAT

Give proper recognition to those widows who are really in need. (1 Tim. 5:3)

In the Early Church, Paul was very concerned that the poor (in this case the widows) were looked after and did not go without. Nowadays a lot of us Christians are fairly well off financially, a roof over our head, a car, nice clothes and a bit of money in the bank. Most of us probably give to the needy and support missions and help those in the poorer parts of the world. Of course this is the right thing to do and we must carry on doing it, but also let's keep looking around in our own church because there may be a "widow" or needy Christian sitting just a few seats away from us. We must give worldwide, but we must never neglect our own either.

Lord, help us to look after any needy Christians that belong to our church.

Do I know any Christians that may need my help?

SUN

CD 1: 25

To act justly and to love mercy ...

(Micah 6:8)

It's so important that we are fair with people and treat them justly. I sometimes meet parents and children's workers who spoil one child while, sometimes not deliberately, ignoring another. Sometimes they give one better presents and spend more time with them, because deep down they get on with them better. This is not good, we must be fair and show equal love and attention at all times. We must also show mercy to people, not retaliation and trying to get revenge. We have all done bad things to hurt God, and there is no reason why He should show His mercy to us yet He does. Why? Because He loves us equally. We must try and be more like Him.

Lord, help us to be fair and show mercy.

Do I treat people fairly?

MON

The Lord said to Moses, "Now the day of your death is near."

(Deut. 31:14)

Most of us have had a loved one or close friend who has died and we've known the sadness that this brings. God wants us to grieve and let the sadness out, and even though that loved one can never be replaced and will always be missed, in time, sadness begins to be replaced by happy memories of the good times we had with that person while they were alive. Moses' time and work on earth was completed and it was now time for him to go and be with God. Of course it would be sad for all his friends left on earth, but for Moses – he was going home. For all Christians living on earth, this world will never be our home, Jesus is preparing our real home in heaven where one day we will live with Him forever.

Lord, it's great to know that our real home is with You.

What do I think my home in heaven will look like?

TUES

Then Peter stood up with the Eleven, raised his voice and addressed the crowd. (Acts 2:14)

This was an amazing day for Peter and his friends. A short while earlier they were scared of saying that they had been friends of Jesus and now, after being filled with the Holy Spirit, Peter was on his feet preaching at the top of his voice. Now, although the words he said were important, what really challenged his listeners was that this fisherman called Peter was so powerful, he was full of the Holy Spirit and anointed by God as he spoke. We will be talking to people today and if we have the chance of sharing the good news of Jesus, let's pray that we too are full of the Holy Spirit when we speak.

Lord, please fill us with Your Holy Spirit today and help us to be powerful for You.

How can I tell the difference between a good speaker and an anointed one?

WEDS

When the people heard this ... they ... said ... "Brothers, what shall we do?" (Acts 2:37)

Yesterday we saw Peter preaching to a very large crowd, today we see how the crowd reacted. The Bible says that they were cut to the heart, in other words they were feeling very guilty that they had done wrong things. "What shall we do?" they asked, and Peter told them that they had to be sorry, turn around and start a new life following Jesus, and be baptised. And 3,000 did just that. I am looking forward to the day when, like Peter's listeners, people are so challenged by what they hear when we preach that they ask us "What shall we do?" I'd love to see 3,000 in my town becoming Christians, wouldn't you?

Lord, we pray many will become Christians in this place where we live.

If 3,000 "seeking" people arrived at our church building next week, what would we do with them?

THURS

In the desert the whole community grumbled against Moses and Aaron.

(Exod. 16:2)

A short while before, the people with Moses and Aaron had been slaves in Egypt and been treated very badly; then they saw the power of the Lord against Pharaoh, they saw the sea open up for them, they saw bad water become pure – and now they grumbled. How could they do such a thing when they had seen God do so much for them? Sadly, quite easily, and they are not a lot different from you and me. We have all seen God do wonderful things in our lives, He's changed us into brand new people and given us a reason for living, yet still we often moan when not everything goes according to our plans. Let's try and stop being grumblers and keep being thankful and praising people.

Lord, please help us not to be grumblers.

What did I last grumble about?

FRI

My eyes grow weak with sorrow; they fail because of all my foes.

(Psa. 6:7)

David was obviously going through a hard time and doing a lot of weeping before God as he prayed. This seemed to not only make his eyes go red, as they do when we cry, but it also seemed to be affecting his vision. I do not cry a lot, although I am sure there are times if I could see things as God sees them that I would be weeping a lot more. I do know, however, that as I get older my eyes are beginning to fail me. Even to write this I need to wear glasses. I pray that even though my eyes may not be able to see things as clearly as they used to, that they will always be able to see what God wants them to see, and not be afraid to weep when God wants them to weep.

Lord, help us not to be afraid to cry.

When did I last cry?

SAT

So you too should be glad and rejoice with me. (Phil. 2:18)

Paul was saying some serious stuff to the Philippians but he also said that he felt glad and rejoiced with all of them and encouraged them to rejoice with him. Yesterday I had a really bad migraine headache and when I get one the last thing that I feel like doing is rejoicing. They sometimes come just before I go on stage to do a "Praise Party", but I would never cancel even though the audience may look one big blur. I am going to praise God and so should they. Let's cheer up and be happy together. It does not always mean that the headache goes instantly, but it certainly seems to go a lot more quickly than if I just sit around feeling sorry for myself.

Lord, help us to encourage others to rejoice and be glad.

How easy do I find it to praise God if I am not feeling well?

Week 26

SUN

CD 1: 26

"Blessed is the king who comes in the name of the Lord." (Luke 19:38)

History is full of all sorts of kings. Some ruled their people very well while others misused their power. Some, to make themselves richer, treated the poor very badly. King Jesus is very different. He loves everyone and yet seems to have a special place in His heart for the poor, the mistreated and the lonely. When King Jesus entered Jerusalem on a donkey people shouted out "Blessed is the King who comes." Jesus is here 2,000 years later, He is still the King and His kingdom is growing larger every day.

Lord, thank You for being the King of kings.

Apart from Jesus, who do I think was the greatest king in the Bible?

MON

The Lord said, "I will surely return ... next year, and Sarah your wife will have a son." (Gen. 18:10)

Abraham was being visited by three messengers from heaven. He fed them and then they suddenly came out with this amazing news. "In a year's time, you and Sarah will have a baby boy." Abraham was surprised by their words as both he and Sarah were far too old to have children, but He knew that when God said something, even though it sounded impossible, He would do it. God still speaks to us today, and a message from God is called a prophecy. We must always be listening out for that word from God and must try not to be too surprised if what He says sounds unlikely or even impossible.

Lord, help us always to be ready to listen to what You have to say.

What was the last prophecy I heard that has now been fulfilled?

TUES

The Lord said ... "Why did Sarah laugh and say, 'Will I really have a child, now that I am old?' " (Gen. 18:13)

Sarah heard the visitors from heaven tell Abraham that she would give birth to a baby boy within a year, she also knew that she was far too old to have children and she laughed, she thought they were joking. We see in our reading that the heavenly visitors had not come to tell jokes, but to bring the word of the Lord and they seemed disappointed that Sarah found it hard to believe that what they said would come true. The next verse says, "Is anything too hard for the Lord?" Let's think about that for a minute: Do we think that anything is too hard for the Lord? Because if we do – we are as unbelieving as Sarah.

Lord, help us to believe that nothing is too hard for You.

How would I have reacted in Sarah's position?

WEDS

"Come, follow me," Jesus said, "and I will make you fishers of men." (Matt. 4:19)

My dad was a keen fisherman and we spent many happy hours on the beach together. I was always amazed every time he opened his fishing bag as it was full of every latest fishing "gimmick" imaginable. Of course none of these helped him to catch fish. It was a bit different with Peter and Andrew, if they did not catch any fish, they would have no income. Fishing was their life, until Jesus came along. People are more important than fish, said Jesus, so put your nets down and follow Me, and they did. It's important that we are always willing to put everything down when Jesus tells us to, so that we can follow Him.

Lord, help us not to let anything get in the way of following You.

What would stop me following Jesus?

THURS

An honest answer is like a kiss on the lips. (Prov. 24:26)

What a wonderful proverb. Kissing someone we love is a beautiful experience for us adults, but maybe some of our little family are not yet of the age to see anything pleasant about a kiss on the lips; in fact to them it may seem quite revolting. With this in mind let's move quickly on to the first part of our verse. God wants us to be honest and to tell the truth. The Bible does not seem to agree with telling half truths or little white lies, it seems God wants us to give honest answers at all times and that is not always easy. However, let's always remember that our honest answers must be shared in love.

Lord, help us always to give honest answers.

Do I like kissing?

FRI

Our God comes and will not be silent ... (Psa. 50:3)

I have a big problem at dinner parties – I find it hard to be quiet. As we sit around the table and everyone is being polite and saying very little, I feel that is my cue to start chatting. Afterwards as we drive home Irene gently reminds me that I did not stop talking for the whole evening. I love talking, and so does God, and I believe that He never stops talking either. He always has so much to say to us His children and nothing and no one will ever silence Him. It must make Him sad when sometimes we are so busy listening to other people that we ignore what He is saying. I talk a lot and sometimes what I say is a load of rubbish, but although God also talks a lot everything He says needs to be listened to.

Lord, thank You that You are never silent and always have things to say to us.

Do I prefer talking or listening?

SAT

All the believers were one in heart and mind. (Acts 4:32)

I have been to many church meetings but I cannot remember one where everyone was one in heart and mind. I hear disagreements over seating, meeting times, leadership, finance and, of course, the Bible. It's good that we can lovingly say how we feel, but it would even be better if we were all so close to the Lord that we knew His mind and plans. Let's take time to hear what God is saying, because I think that He is saying similar things to each of us.

Lord, please help us to be one in heart and mind with our fellow believers.

When was the last time that I disagreed with a decision made in my church?

SUN

CD 2: 1

... Put on the full armour of God so that you can ... stand against the devil's schemes ... (Eph. 6:10-17).

As much as we all hate wars, the Bible tells us that they will go on happening until the Lord Jesus comes back again. Picture a soldier on the battlefront, facing the enemy without any weapons or protection. He is going to get hurt. God has given us weapons and armour to wear, not to hurt people but to fight against bad things and protect ourselves from the devil's destructive plans. If we live our lives without wearing God's armour we too are going to get badly hurt. Let's keep hold of the sword of the Spirit and wear God's armour at all times.

Lord, help us never to forget to wear the armour of God.

What armour of God do I most forget to wear?

MON

No-one claimed that any of his possessions was his own, but they shared everything they had. (Acts 4:32)

As a little boy I was part of a Christian community that lived in a similar way to our scripture. Everyone gave up everything and both adults and children were given £1 each week as pocket money to buy little luxuries like chocolate, sweets etc. Of course £1 was worth a lot more in those days. We all lived in a big house, ate together, had meetings together and worked on the 11-acre farm together and no one was richer or poorer than anyone else. I was surrounded by uncles and aunties and I really enjoyed this way of living. I imagine heaven will be similar. We will all be one big happy family worshipping God, and money and possessions will mean absolutely nothing. I like the thought of that.

Lord, thank You that we are part of a wonderful Christian family.

Do I like sharing my possessions with others, even if I do not get them back?

TUES

"As surely as the Lord lives and as you live, I will not leave you." (2 Kings 2:2)

Elisha was walking with an older man of God called Elijah whom he greatly respected and admired. Three times Elijah gave him the chance to leave him, and three times Elisha gave the reply of our Scripture verse. Elisha knew there were things he could learn from Elijah and he was going to stay with him until the end. I have a friend who is an ageing man of God whom I greatly admire and I just love to spend time with him. He is not perfect, but I know that every time I leave his house I am richer spiritually, and have learned more about God. It's good to find Elijahs – older men and women of God with whom we can spend time and maybe gather a bit of their anointing and wisdom.

Lord, thank You for older and wiser Christians, help us to learn from them.

Who could I go to for encouragement?

WEDS

I also want women to dress modestly, with decency and propriety ... (1 Tim. 2:9)

We must remember that Paul was not God. When he writes to churches he is not setting out more laws and commandments, he is often just giving good common sense advice that he feels will be helpful. In our Scripture verse Paul is not entering into the world of the female fashion critic and he was not saying that women should not dress attractively, but he is saying that women should think about what they are wearing. As believers, none of us should be wanting to attract everyone's eyes onto us. It should be that in all we do, say and wear, that we are wanting people to fix their eyes on Jesus.

Lord, thank You for clothes, help us to wear the appropriate ones for each occasion.

Have I any clothes that may not be "appropriate"?

THURS All your words are true.

(Psa. 119:160)

Part of me is an evangelist. This simply means that I love telling people of all ages about the good news of Jesus. Sadly, we evangelists have got a reputation for exaggerating or "adding to" the truth. This usually happens when numbers are quoted referring to the amount of people who attended meetings or those who said they would like to follow Jesus. The larger the number, the better it makes us look. All God's words are true and He wants all the words that we say to be really truthful, without exaggeration or made-up stories. Let's think before we say or write something. We do not need to impress anyone, except God, and He is only impressed when we tell the truth.

Lord, please help us to tell the truth.

When was the last time that I exaggerated a story?

FRI If you have not been trustworthy in ... worldly wealth, who will trust you with true riches?" (Luke 16:11)

It's not the amount of money we have that is important, it's what we do with that money that will prove if we are trustworthy. Some earn wages, some are given pocket money but if we waste what we are given, be it a large or small amount, we cannot expect God to believe that we are ready to receive riches of greater value. Now this does not mean that we should not be generous with what we have, or that we cannot spend some of it on little luxuries; it means as Christians that we ask God how we should spend it, or who we should give it to. This applies to boys and girls as much as men and women. When we can prove that we are trustworthy with our money ... then will come the true riches from heaven.

Lord help us to be trustworthy with our money.

Can I be trusted with money?

SAT

He spreads the snow like wool ...

(Psa. 147:16)

I live on the south coast of England and we rarely have much snow, but on my travels I come across a lot of the fluffy white stuff. I remember one winter I was in Winnipeg in Canada and I went to sleep with no snow, but when I woke up – we were completely snowed in and I could not get to my arranged bookings. Everything looked pure and clean and it sparkled. It is as the psalmist said, God spreads the snow like wool, and it's yet another part of God's creative beauty that we can enjoy.

Lord, thank You for the beauty that can be seen in freshly fallen snow.

Do I like snow?

Week 28

SUN

CD 2: 2

"... the grass withers and the flowers fall, but the word of the Lord stands forever." (1 Pet. 1:24-25)

Sometimes, even in Britain, the rain stops falling and the sun begins to shine. On rare occasions we can even have wonderful sunshine with no rain for a few weeks! In my garden I have a large amount of grass (not lawn, as its full of weeds and moss). At the front of the house are Irene's hanging baskets containing some beautiful flowers. However, every year, when the rain stops and if we forget to water them, in a very short time the grass becomes bleached and the flowers look terribly wilted. It's great to know that God's Word does not depend on the weather or indeed anything else. It is totally reliable, dependable and unchanging every single day.

Lord, thank You that Your Word is unchanging.

How can I help conserve water to help my country in dry seasons?

MON

"God opposes the proud but gives grace to the humble." (1 Pet. 5:5)

I enjoy standing on a large stage in front of hundreds, sometimes thousands, of people and watching their happy faces as they applaud what I have done. That is when I have to watch out that I do not become proud. Sometimes organisers introduce me as "one of Britain's leading children's workers" and although I know they are trying to be nice, I just have to ignore what they are saying, because the minute I start believing my own publicity I know that God will not be happy with His proud servant. We must all beware the dangers of this thing called pride, as it does not just affect people who spend a lot of their lives on stages.

Lord, help us not to be proud.

When was the last time that I felt proud?

TUES

Do not gloat when your enemy falls; when he stumbles, do not let your heart rejoice. (Prov. 24:17)

People often say things that hurt me and, although I know I must love them and forgive them, I do find it very hard to forget what they have said. Sometimes later I hear that something has gone wrong in their life and my initial response is that it serves them right or, worse still, I think that God is punishing them for the hurt they caused me. Sadly, sometimes I even feel good when I hear that things have turned bad for them. I must ask God to forgive me for feeling this way as our scripture tells us we should never gloat or rejoice when even an enemy gets into bad times.

Lord help us never to gloat over others' misfortunes.

Can I think of a time when I was happy because of other people's misfortunes?

WEDS

The baby leaped in her womb, and Elizabeth was filled with the Holy Spirit. (Luke 1:41)

I love seeing pregnant women at my meetings because although I only see one chair filled, I know there are two people sitting on it and two people who are going to feel the presence of God. The little life in the womb enjoys being in the presence of praising Christians just as John the Baptist in Elizabeth's tummy could not resist having a good old jump for joy when Jesus appeared in His mum, Mary's tummy. Let's never forget these little ones enjoy the presence of Jesus long before they come into this world, and lets regularly pray for both mother and baby.

Lord, help us to pray for these new little lives even before they enter our world.

How much do I think unborn babies can know and feel?

THURS

Gideon replied, "If now I have found favour in your eyes, give me a sign ... " (Judg. 6:17)

As a young Christian I was never sure if I was doing something because the Lord wanted me to do it or if it was just an idea of mine that I wanted the Lord to be part of. I would often put out a "Gideon fleece" to confirm that it was God not me. After a while I found that asking for a sign was showing a lack of faith. What I needed to do was to spend more time with God and the Bible and get to recognise His voice. Jesus said that His sheep know His voice, but even sheep have to listen.

Lord, help us to listen to You and not always need to be looking for signs.

Have I ever asked God to give me a sign?

FRI

Then Joshua sent the people away, each to his own inheritance.

(Josh. 24:28)

An inheritance is not something we have to work for, or ask for, it is something that is passed on to us by someone who cares for us. What usually happens is that when someone dies their will is read out. Many people suddenly become wealthy if a rich person has left them a lot of money. I remember when my Dad died, amongst other things he left me some of his books that he knew I would enjoy, and his fishing rods – because he knew that I liked fishing, but best of all, he left me wonderful memories. I think leaving behind memories of a loving, godly life, is much more important than just passing on material possessions. Possessions will soon rot away but memories of our examples as men and women of God won't.

Lord, help us to be good examples of followers of Jesus.

What am I most looking forward to inheriting?

SAT

"The kingdom of heaven is like treasure hidden in a field."

(Matt. 13:44)

The man in our story actually found the treasure in someone else's field. For it to be his, he sold everything he had so he could afford to buy the field and of course have the treasure that was buried in it. When I bought my last car I had to hand over my old one in part exchange. We had spent many thousands of happy miles travelling together. However, there could be no room for sentimentality as there was no way that I could afford the newer one without selling the old one first. The greatest treasure on earth is Jesus, and to receive the life that He has for us will mean giving up everything that we have.

Lord, You are the greatest treasure we can have.

Would I have told the owner about the treasure in his field before I bought it off him?

SUN

CD 2: 3

"Why do you look for the living among the dead?" (Luke 24:5)

Very old church buildings seem to be surrounded by reminders of the dead. The graveyard is full of sad grey obelisks, there are stone tombs in the building, plaques on the walls naming those who have passed away, and a cross at the front with someone who is supposed to resemble a dead Jesus hanging on it. It is sometimes like looking for the living among the dead. But Jesus is not here, He's alive. He is no longer on a cross or in a tomb or graveyard, He is sitting with His Father in heaven. Christianity is about being forever thankful for the death of Jesus, and even more thankful that He is alive today.

Lord, thank You for being alive today.

Can I really praise a living Jesus when surrounded by so many reminders of the dead?

MON

David continued up the Mount of Olives, weeping as he went. (2 Sam. 15:30)

David loved and trusted his children. One day, however, his son Absalom decided that he wanted to take his dad's place and become king, so he conspired against David and took over the palace in Jerusalem. David was heartbroken as we can see from our reading, but rather than cause trouble he and his subjects moved out of the city. Later on Absalom came to a very sad end, but David never stopped loving him. Mothers and fathers are often hurt by what their children say or do but because our children are a gift from God, like King David, we can never stop loving them.

Lord help us to love our family not just in words but in action.

If I were David, would I have acted differently?

TUES Then they accompanied him to the ship. (Acts 20:38)

I am terrible in ships and boats. I remember I was once going to speak on the island of Jersey and decided to go by boat. For a while everything was fine, then suddenly a storm began, the sea became rough and I was very sick for the rest of the voyage. In Paul's day, ships were the only way to cross water and Paul not only sailed on rough seas, he also knew what it was to be shipwrecked. He would never let rough seas stop him from taking the message of Jesus to others, however, and although the trips may not have been pleasant, the opportunity to pass on the good news always made them worthwhile. Myself, I thank the Lord for the invention of planes.

Lord, thank You for transport and the opportunity of being able to take Your good news to all parts of the globe.

What is my favourite mode of transport?

WEDS When his master heard the story his wife told him ... he burned with anger. (Gen. 39:19)

Poor Joseph, in the wrong place at the wrong time. Potiphar's wife was a horrible woman who told her husband that Joseph fancied her, when he obviously didn't and, sadly, the husband believed his lying wife and Joseph was in trouble. There may be times when you and I are accused of doing things which are untrue and, sadly, there are always those around who want to believe the worst about us. Let's not get involved in a big argument. We just need to state our innocence and leave it with God who knows the truth and will always stand by the innocent.

Lord, help us to still love those who accuse us of things that we haven't done.

Is there someone I always believe the worst about, even if it may not be true?

THURS

Do not be carried away by all kinds of strange teachings. (Heb. 13:9)

When I teach from the Bible, I encourage people to check the Word for themselves to make sure that what I am saying is true. Nowadays there are still those who teach strange things, and those who blindly accept the things they are being taught. It gets worse if the listener gets "carried away" by this strange teaching and starts insisting that others also believe it. This can be dangerous. We must check out all we are taught with the Bible. That is where we will always discover what is true.

Lord, help us to think about what we are being taught, and to check it out with the Bible.

When did I last hear some strange teaching, and did I check it out?

FRI

"For where two or three come together in my name, there am I with them." (Matt. 18:20)

Church is not a building that Christians meet in. Church is not a meeting on Sunday, and nobody ever "goes" to church. Church is often described as the Body of Jesus on earth. Another way to think of Church is when two or three people who love Jesus meet together. One person cannot be the Church, although they can of course be part of the Church. With this in mind, we can see how important it is that we regularly meet up with other believers because, as our Scripture reading says, that is where we are going to find Jesus.

Lord, thank You that we are part of Your Church.

What do I think Church is?

SAT

There is the sea, vast and spacious, teeming with creatures beyond number. (Psa. 104:25)

I am not the world's greatest swimmer, and I soon get bored with waggling my arms and legs about in water just to stay afloat, especially in a swimming pool. Now the sea is different. I have often visited other countries where the weather (and the water) is a lot warmer than in the UK. I love to swim out in the sea with goggles on and look at all the fish swimming around me; they are so beautiful. We can never really imagine how vast the seas are, let alone how many millions of creatures live in them, all with individual colours. It's amazing, God knows every one of them; well, He must do, He made them all.

Lord, thank You for all the creatures that live in the sea.

Why do I enjoy (or not enjoy) the seaside?

Week 30

SUN

CD 2: 4

"Neither do people light a lamp and put it under a bowl." (Matt. 5:15)

It would be very silly to get a torch, go into a dark place where we want to be able to see and then cover our torch with a bucket. It would stop all the light and we would still be in the dark. Jesus says that when we love Him we are like His lights in a dark world, so we should never hide the fact that we are Christians. It's not that we just walk round preaching at everyone – we should be shining out God's light by the things that we do and the people we are. It's when people see our changed lives that they will want to know about Jesus.

Lord, help us never to hide our light or be scared to admit that we are Christians.

What can others see in my life, that points them to Jesus?

MON

Peter ... asked, "Lord, how many times shall I forgive my brother ... ?" (Matt. 18:21)

When my children were little, if they did something wrong, I would tell them off and warn them not to do it again. I felt very sad if after a short while they did the same thing again and if they ever did it a third time I would be very upset and sometimes even a little angry. I am so glad that Jesus is not like me. I realise that often I do the same sin over and over again, and the wonderful news is that He will never stop forgiving me. Of course this does not mean that I should not worry about doing wrong, of course I should, but it does mean that Jesus never stops loving me even when I do things that make Him sad.

Lord, thank You for always being willing to forgive the wrong things that we do and say.

How often could I forgive someone before I would not want them to be my friend anymore?

TUES

The wings of the ostrich flap joyfully ... (Job 39:13)

It's strange but nowadays when we think of ostriches we rarely think of them flapping joyful wings as in our Scripture reading. We would probably think of a rather silly bird that buries its head in the sand when it meets any problems thinking that by the time it takes its head out of the sand the problem will have disappeared. We must never be like that. When we face difficulties and problems we must learn to take them to Jesus and tell Him all about them, it's only then that He will lead us through them and even help us to rejoice while we face them.

Lord, thank You for ostriches, but help us never try to hide away from our problems.

When did I last try and hide away from a problem?

WEDS Until I come, devote yourself to the public reading of Scripture ... (1 Tim. 4:13)

Paul gives young Timothy advice and encourages him to commit himself to reading the Scriptures out loud to others so that they can learn more of God and His wonderful love. It's great that we can have our own Bibles and, if we choose to, we can spend time by ourselves reading them. It is also good to take it in turns to read the Bible out loud to each other so while one reads the others can listen and take in what is being read to them. We see it happening in most church meetings; it's also worth doing in our homes.

Lord, thank You that we can read the Bible to others and help them know more about You.

Do I prefer to read the Bible myself, or have it read to me?

THURS "I the Lord search the heart and examine the mind ..." (Jer. 17:10)

It's easy for me to say things to people that I know they want to hear. However, sometimes I do not mean it, other times I am not even thinking about what I am saying, I'm thinking of something else entirely. In these cases I am just saying words and even though they may encourage my listener, they are meaningless. God is not just interested in what I say, He is also interested in what is going on in my heart and my mind and of course He knows exactly how I am really feeling and what I am really thinking.

Lord, I realise You can see all that we are thinking and feeling. Please help us to mean the words we say.

What can God see in my heart and mind, now?

FRI

Jesus [said], "... one of you is going to betray me." (John 13:21)

Friends are very important, but friends can let you down and even break your heart. Jesus had chosen twelve special friends and for three years He had grown close to them, taught them, cared for them and shown them some wonderful miracles. They must have known that Jesus was very different from any other person because they had never heard or seen Him do anything wrong. Sadly, one of those friends was going to turn on Him and treat Him worse than an enemy. We can never imagine how sad Jesus must have felt when this happened.

" **Lord, please help us to be loyal to our friends.**

? **Have I broken any of my friends' hearts?**

SAT

Elisha said, "Hear the word of the Lord." (2 Kings 7:1)

Many of us have been to meetings where someone has told us that they have come to bring us a word from the Lord. We listen eagerly and wait to see what we can learn from what is being said. Elisha was a bit different. When he had a word from the Lord he often gave it to the most important person of the day, the king. God has things to say to us in meetings, but He also has things to say to the people who are in charge of running our country. Let's pray God raises up some Elishas today who have a word from the Lord and the courage to pass it on to those in positions who can change things for the better.

" **Lord, we pray for our country's leaders. We pray they may hear Your voice.**

? **Who is the most important person I have ever talked to?**

SUN

CD 2: 5

Better a poor but wise youth than an old but foolish king ... (Eccl. 4:13)

A few years ago, one of my younger team members warned one of my older team members about how careful they should be when playing physical games with children. The older team member reacted very badly to this, thinking that, due to age and experience, this younger adviser had no right to give an older person such warnings. None of us are ever too old to be warned and if we refuse to listen to the people advising us, whatever age they are, we are very foolish and heading for big trouble.

Lord, help us always to be open to receive warnings and advice.

Would I listen to advice from someone who is a lot younger than me?

MON

All the days ordained for me were written in your book. (Psa. 139:16)

Bible teachers have discussed this for centuries. Has God planned my life for me, and if He has, does that mean I have no choice as to what I do and don't do? Maybe it's not that complicated. God has given us the opportunity to choose what we do, sometimes we do what is right and sometimes we do what is wrong. He would never take the freedom to choose away from us.
But God is God, and being God He must know everything. This means that He knows all the choices that we are going to make in our lives, but He does not make them for us. Let's try and choose to do the right things that we know will please Almighty God.

Lord, help us to choose to do what is right.

Does God really know everything about me?

TUES Miriam ... took a tambourine ... and all the women followed her ... dancing. (Exod. 15:20)

Miriam, Aaron's sister, was enjoying giving thanks to the Lord with all the other women. They danced and played that jingly percussion instrument called a tambourine. A lot of celebrations that I attend have banned the tambourine for a couple of reasons. The first is: if it is played out of time it's hard for the musicians to play in time, and the second is that if the meeting is being recorded it can spoil it for the listener. I can understand these points, but I think that sometimes we should consider the player who is getting blessed and not just the listener who isn't. The Bible talks about making a joyful noise and does not mention that it has to be either in tune or in time.

Lord, show us different ways that we can give thanks to You.

Should I be allowed to praise God in any way I choose?

WEDS Dear friends, now we are children of God ... (1 John 3:2)

One of my sons once said to me, "Dad, you are not like other dads, you have never really grown up have you, you are more like a friend than a dad." I did not mind this comment because although my children of course know I am their dad, they also see me as a friend who enjoys listening, watching and even taking part in the same things that they do. The Bible never says that Christians become adult, we just grow to become more mature children of God. Being children means that, whatever age we are, we will always be full of fun, very excitable and totally dependent on our Heavenly Father.

Lord, it's great being a child of Yours.

Do I have to enjoy playing games with children?

THURS

It took Solomon thirteen years, however, to complete the construction of his palace. (1 Kings 7:1)

In the verse before today's verse we read that Solomon had spent seven years building God's house, the Temple. It's interesting to note the word "however" in today's verse; in other words Solomon spent nearly twice as long building his own house as he did building God's. Today, sadly, we are no different. Although we say we love the Lord, we spend far more time thinking about our families, our possessions and even watching TV than we do thinking about God. God knows our faults, and the wonderful thing is that He loves us anyway, but let's make the effort to try and give Him a greater place in our time and our lives.

Lord, please help us to give You a greater place in our lives.

Should our church buildings be as nice or even nicer than the houses we live in?

FRI

"Ask him. He is of age; he will speak for himself." (John 9:21)

Those Pharisees certainly knew how to spoil a party. Jesus had just healed a man who was born blind. Just think how excited and thrilled his parents must have felt. Then along came the Pharisees, like wet blankets, to question the parents because they did not want to believe that Jesus was God's Son or that He was capable of performing such miracles. The parents lived in fear of the Pharisees, and soon all the excitement was overcome by fear. We must not be frightened of anyone. Jesus still does wonderful things in our lives every day, let's never be scared to tell people that it's Jesus who is the One who cares for us and looks after all our needs.

Lord, help us not to be frightened to tell people about all the wonderful things that You do for us.

Am I frightened of any Christians?

SAT

A champion named Goliath, who was from Gath, came out of the Philistine camp. (1 Sam. 17:4)

There is no doubt about it, this guy was seriously big, big enough to scare the whole Israelite army, but he was still only a man. All the other Philistine soldiers around him would have been just normal size, so it's hard to see why everyone was so scared of just one human big guy. Today we can allow problems to become giants and feel that these giants are impossible to conquer. Really they are no different to any other problem that is facing us, but they just look bigger. All giants look very small if we ask Almighty God who holds the universe in His hands to come and deal with them. Let's never forget that.

Lord, please help us to sort out both our big and small problems.

What is my biggest problem today?

Week 32

SUN

CD 2: 6

We do not want you to become lazy … (Heb. 6:12)

Sleep and rest are essential and we know that even the perfect body of the Lord Jesus needed times for both. But we do have to be careful. Our time on earth is limited and God has plans for us to fulfil and a mission for us to complete. This means that we must watch out that we do not become lazy by spending too many hours in bed, or too much time watching TV or playing computer games when there are much more important things that we could and should be doing. TVs and computers are great inventions if used in small doses, but spending too much precious time with these entertainments can easily bring about laziness.

Lord, help us not to become lazy.

What do I do that makes me lazy?

MON

The king said to the girl, "Ask me for anything you want, and I'll give it to you." (Mark 6:22)

King Herod had done many wrong things and John the Baptist had never been frightened to point these things out to both him and the queen. Here, King Herod is at a party where he has eaten and drunk too much and, after enjoying watching the queen's daughter dancing, told her that she could have anything she wanted, and he would give it to her. Her mother told her to ask for John the Baptist to be killed. The king was upset but felt he had to kill John because he had made a promise. Let's be very careful what we promise people, especially if we are feeling very excited and are with friends who are not Christians. They may want us to do things that later we might regret doing.

“” **Lord, please help us not make any promises that could lead us into doing wrong things.**

? **Have I made any silly promises lately?**

TUES

Such knowledge is too wonderful for me ... (Psa. 139:6)

This must be one of my favourite psalms and in it King David explains how God is way beyond his human thinking. He is amazed that God knows everything about him and he is also well aware that there is nowhere he could go in the whole of the universe where God could not see him or find him. Sometimes I think we forget how big and powerful God really is and this happens because we just think of Him as being one of our best friends. Awesome is a great old-fashioned word to help define God – it means overwhelming wonder and admiration. We should always be in awe of God.

“” **Lord, when we think of You we are filled with overwhelming wonder and admiration.**

? **Let me try and explain how big God is.**

WEDS

"You have heard that it was said, "Eye for eye, and tooth for tooth." (Matt. 5:38)

Jesus taught a whole new way of thinking. In the Old Testament, as we can see in our reading, if someone punched you in the eye or smacked you in the mouth, you had every right to retaliate by doing the same to them. Jesus said that He did not want His followers to retaliate or fight back. He wants us to return love for aggression and hatred. Of course this is very hard to do as it seems to go against our normal reactions, but we know that this was the example Jesus set us and this is the way He wants us to act. We will need to ask Him to help us to be able to love our enemies as it not the easiest thing to do.

Lord, help us to be able to turn the other cheek and not to fight back.

Who are my enemies, and can I love them?

THURS

A time to be silent and a time to speak. (Eccl. 3:7)

I love talking. Sometimes I go with some friends for a round of golf. Now I am not very good at golf, but I love walking around the beautiful countryside and I also love chatting to my friends as we play. Of course if I continue talking while someone is about to hit a ball everyone goes "Shhhh!" and tells me to be quiet as the player is trying to concentrate. I also love talking to God, but I have learned that although He never says shhhh, He too sometimes likes me to be quiet, otherwise I will never listen to what He is saying to me.

Lord, help us to know when to speak and when to be silent.

What sports do I enjoy where at times I have to be quiet?

FRI

"Then they gave me the gold, and I threw it into the fire, and out came this calf!" (Exod. 32:24)

It's very easy to make up stories and say things that may not be strictly true, but Aaron is the limit. Does he really think that Moses is going to believe that he threw the Israelites' gold jewellery onto a fire and a golden calf popped out? Doing wrong things is bad enough, but then to tell such a blatent lie makes things even worse. When I was very little I had a few imaginary friends, one I called Africa. When I did something wrong and my mother caught me I would tell her that it wasn't me who did it, it was Africa. It's funny, but she never believed that Africa was to blame. When we do wrong we must own up and admit it.

Lord, help us to own up when we do wrong things.

Do I feel bad when I tell a lie?

SAT

He said, "Whoever is for the Lord, come to me." (Exod. 32:26)

We all have to make decisions. Some people would love it if a member of the family, a friend or even a church leader made decisions for them. Life would be so much easier. The Israelites had sinned against God by worshipping this golden calf and Moses said they had to make a decision. If they really wanted to follow God they had to stand with him. Some did, and some chose not to. Supposing Moses said the same words to us today, would we stand with him? If we choose to live for Jesus let's try to live for Him 100 per cent, and put Him first in everything.

Lord, we choose to live for You, please help us to do it.

If I was with unsaved friends and asked to put my hand up if I was a Christian, would I do it?

SUN

CD 2: 7

I have become all things to all men ... (1 Cor. 9:22)

Although Paul may have upset people with some of the things he said, he never wanted to offend anyone by the things he did or even the things he ate. He felt that, whenever possible, it was far more important to please them than just do things to please himself, because by doing this, he might have more opportunities to pass on the Christian message. I love eating meat, but if I invite vegetarians for a meal, to show love to them, I will not put meat on the table. There are lots of things that we can enjoy without sinning, but we still do not want to do anything that may offend those who are not yet Christians.

Lord, help us not to cause offence to those who do not yet know You.

When I entertain people, do I eat what they like, or expect them to eat what I enjoy?

MON

Then their eyes were opened and they recognised him.

(Luke 24:31)

Jesus had been crucified and while some of His friends believed that He had come back to life, some didn't. Here, two of Jesus' best friends are walking along the road talking to the resurrected Christ but not recognising Him until He gives thanks for some bread and hands it to them. These guys were not looking for something special or a miracle, they were just getting on with their ordinary lives. Nowadays, Jesus may not appear to us so we can see Him with our eyes, but every day He is with us and does wonderful things for us. I wonder how often we recognise that it is Jesus who is with us and caring for us? Let's keep our eyes wide open; we will see that He is involved with us all day long.

Lord, help us to recognise that You are with us all through the day.

I wonder why Jesus' friends did not recognise Him earlier?

TUES "Follow me," Jesus told him, and Levi got up and followed him. (Mark 2:14)

Matthew [Levi] had a very good job collecting taxes. Although many people may not have liked him for the career he had chosen, in all probability he was set up for life with a regular income. Then along came Jesus. We do not hear that Jesus had a long conversation with Matthew, or even promised him a better job, He just simply said "Follow me" and immediately Matthew did so. Jesus stills calls us to follow Him today. For some, it will be to follow Him as we study or as we work, for others it will be to follow Him with no promise of any income except to trust Him that He will provide all our needs. Either way Jesus has said these words at one time or another to all believers, "Follow me."

Lord, help us to always follow You.

What do I think is the worst job in the world?

WEDS Then Abram gave him a tenth of everything. (Gen. 14:20)

Here we have one of the first mentions of giving a tenth, which nowadays in church life is called a tithe. Abraham gave it to Melchizedek, and all we know about him is that he was the king of Salem, and the priest of God Most High. Certainly Abraham must have thought he was very special, to give him a tenth of all he owned. Nowadays we are encouraged to give a tenth of our income to our local church as a minimum of our giving. Some agree with this, others may not, but let's never forget that Jesus today does not want just a tenth of what we have as everything we have should already belong to Him. All we possess is on loan from Jesus so that should make it easier to give everything away, if He wants us to.

Lord, You own everything we have.

Should I give a tenth of my money to my local church?

THURS

You were running a good race. Who cut in on you and kept you from obeying the truth? (Gal. 5:7)

I was never a great runner but I would always give it a go. Running in set lanes looks quite straightforward, but it can be very frustrating if you are running well and another runner cuts in front of you and obstructs you, causing your pace to slow. The Galatians were obviously running well for Jesus until someone cut across them and slowed them down by telling them lies. We must beware of this today. The real truth only comes from God's Word and if someone tries to pass on "good ideas" that are not part of the Bible, we had better watch out. If these are lies they will slow down and mess up the "race we are running" for Jesus.

Lord, please help us to keep running the Christian "race" for You.

How do I react if someone pushes in front of me in a queue?

FRI

"... who ... puts [my words] into practice is like a wise man who built his house on the rock." (Matt. 7:24)

The story of the wise and foolish men is not really a children's story – it is very frightening. Jesus said that if we follow Him, it is like building our lives on solid rock (and He is that solid rock). If we don't, and we choose to build our lives on anything else, it's like building our lives on sand and when the rains and floods come our houses will collapse upon us. I guess this story should make us all the more thankful that we are followers of Jesus, and all the more urgent in telling our friends who may be living on the sand, the good news of Jesus.

Lord, it's great to live on the rock; help us to pass on Your good news to those who live on the sand.

Are there stories in the Bible that I would not tell young children?

SAT

As Solomon grew old, his wives turned his heart after other gods ... (1 Kings 11:4)

Solomon may have been one of the wisest guys ever, but was he wise when he chose to marry 700 wives of royal birth plus have 300 special lady friends? He thought that to marry all these royal ladies from other nations would bring peace and prosperity to his kingdom, but he seemed to ignore the fact they worshipped other gods, bringing these into his palace. We should be peacemakers but not at the cost of going against God's Word. How sad that God's friend, Solomon, in the end allowed himself to be led the wrong way. Let's never forget there is only one true God whom we should love and serve.

Lord, make us wiser than Solomon, and never allow people to lead us away from you.

What problems would having so many wives bring?

Week 34

SUN

CD 2: 8

Taking the five loaves and the two fish and looking up to heaven, he gave thanks ... (Luke 9:16-17)

There are so many good things that God does for us and gives to us that we never thank Him for. I really think it is good, before we eat, to give thanks for both the food and those who have prepared it for us. I do not suggest you need to close your eyes to pray. I remember being on a youth camp and when I closed my eyes to give thanks, someone stole one of my sausages! As we give thanks, let's look at the food and the chef and praise God for both of them.

Lord, help us always to give thanks for the wonderful food You provide for us to eat.

Should I give thanks for my food out loud if I am in a restaurant?

MON

Those controlled by the sinful nature cannot please God. (Rom. 8:8)

There are certain times and places when I know I am more likely to allow my old sinful nature to come and control me. For me it's usually when I am feeling very tired and, strangely enough, usually when I have been involved in something where God has really blessed me. It's at these times I try and avoid being in certain places and doing certain things because, although my sinful nature may please me for a short while, I know that it does not please God. I'm a new person, I do not want to let my old nature ever to take control again, and I am going to do all I can not to let it.

Lord, please help us not to allow our old nature to take control.

Is there anything in my life that I cannot control?

TUES

Much dreaming and many words are meaningless. Therefore stand in awe of God. (Eccl. 5:7)

It's strange how some people never seem to dream, yet every night I dream about something or other. Most of my dreams are meaningless and rubbish and I forget them very quickly, but occasionally God speaks to me in a dream and in the morning it is very clearly in my mind. Once I dreamt up a song and it was so vivid, I had to get up in the middle of the night and go downstairs and sing it into a cassette recorder as I was frightened that I would forget it by the morning. One little warning, though, we must be careful what we watch on TV or what we read before we go to sleep, because sometimes these can cause horrid dreams.

Lord, when we dream, please help our dreams to be nice ones.

Can I remember a nice dream that I have had?

WEDS

"Take the first fish you catch ... and you will find a ... coin ... for my tax and yours." (Matt. 17:27)

The tax collectors were after Jesus and His friends, wanting them to pay the Temple tax. Jesus decided He did not want to offend them and that it was right to pay it, but look where He got the coin from. He told Peter to go fishing, and in the mouth of the first fish that he caught, he found enough money to pay both Jesus' and the disciples' taxes. I wonder how often we worry about money, even money to pay our taxes. Let's not worry, it's the same Jesus we serve today who put the coin into the fish's mouth. If we stay close to Him, He will look after us and will sometimes provide in miraculous ways – I'm off fishing!

Lord, thank You that You provide enough money to even pay our taxes.

If someone gives me more money than they should in change, do I tell them or do I keep the money?

THURS

It is unthinkable that God would do wrong ... (Job 34:12)

It is not only unthinkable, it is the greatest impossibility in the world. God is perfect in every way and He could never ever do any wrong thing and we believe that don't we? Our newspapers are full of writers blaming God for every war, every famine, in fact every terrible thing that happens. Note that the same writers never thank Him when there is good news and things are going well! But we Christians need to be careful. Sometimes God does not answer our prayers in the way we would like Him to, and we accuse Him of not listening or even not caring when maybe someone we love is in great pain but does not get healed. We do not understand some of God's decisions but we must believe that He always makes the right ones – He can do no wrong.

Lord, You are God, You can never do any wrong thing.

Have I prayed a prayer that God has not answered?

FRI

Now to the King eternal ... the only God, be honour and glory for ever and ever. (1 Tim. 1:17)

King Jesus is eternal and immortal. All around us are things that over a short period of time will either rust, decay or fall to bits. King Jesus has no beginning and no end, He has been and will be around for ever. He is invisible; we can't see Him with our eyes, but we know that He is always with us. He is the only God. Some people worship gods with other names and some have made gods out of their homes, families or possessions. But there is only one true God and we should honour Him and give Him our thanks forever.

Lord, thank You for being our King and our God.

If God is invisible, how do I know He is with me?

SAT

Praise be to the Lord, to God our Saviour, who daily bears our burdens. (Psa. 68:19)

When I was young, and very fit and healthy, I worked on a farm. The corn and animal food would arrive in very heavy sacks and we would often have a competition to see who could carry a very heavy sack on his back for the longest time. It was hard work, and no one smiled as they were competing. We all tend to carry burdens, although not through choice and not sacks of corn. We are burdened by tough times at school and work, problems in the home and relationships, money – or lack of it – and so I could go on. The good news is we need not walk around struggling with those great heavy burdens, the Lord says He is willing to take them from us so we can be free and happy again.

Lord, please release us from any burdens that are weighing us down.

Am I carrying a burden that I need to give to Jesus?

SUN

CD 2: 9

So whether you eat or drink or whatever you do, do it all for the glory of God. (1 Cor. 10:31)

We must always be aware of those around us who may stumble or be upset if we do or say things which are not helpful to them. When I was a small boy I once had breakfast with a Jew. Now for some strange reason I remember telling him how much I enjoyed black pudding. All at the table stopped eating, went quiet and stared at me. This Jew was a very kind and godly man and realised that I had not said this to offend him. He then, with a big grin on his face and with my parents' permission, explained to me that he did not eat black pudding and that it was made out of pig's blood. Yuk, I had no idea. We give glory to God for all food and drink, but we still must consider others with different viewpoints.

Lord, help us not to do things that may offend others.

Is there any food that I could not eat because I know where it has come from?

MON

God ... who comforts us in all our troubles, so that we can comfort those in any trouble ... (2 Cor. 1:4)

Everyone has troubles and difficult times, and we all need someone we can turn to who will comfort us. A wonderful thing about being a Christian is that we know beyond a shadow of doubt that our Heavenly Father God is always available to be our Comforter. But our verse does not end there. When we have been comforted by Father God, we then should be able to go up to our friends who are in trouble and comfort them, especially friends who might not yet be Christians. As they feel the love we show them, let's pray for opportunities to share with them who gave us that love and compassion – Father God.

Lord, help us to be able to comfort those in trouble

Who have I comforted lately?

TUES They laughed at him, knowing that she was dead. (Luke 8:53)

Laughter is a very strange thing. Jesus arrives at the house of a little girl who has sadly died and says that she is not dead, just sleeping. Some of the mourners mock Jesus and burst into laughter as though He has told some sort of joke. It would be understandable if they argued with Him and told Him that He was wrong and that she was definitely dead – but to laugh!
We must be careful when we laugh, if it's something funny let's all have a good laugh together, but if we are laughing in mockery, that is not good. Anyway, Jesus and the parents had the last laugh because Jesus brought the little girl back to life again.

Lord, please help us not to laugh at people.

Have I ever mocked someone?

WEDS Their venom is like the venom of a snake ... (Psa. 58:4)

King David is likening the evil of the wicked to the poisonous venom of a snake. I do not like snakes much and, although I have never been bitten by one, on one of my trips to Arkansas, I was bitten on the foot by a very venomous spider called the brown recluse. I will never forget it; one of the church leaders asked me to take off my sock and shoe, then he spat on my foot and prayed. God wonderfully healed me and I soon felt great again. I was told that the venom from this spider could really damage the body. Wicked people can also cause damage, but we still must pray for them, they are not beyond saving and Jesus still loves them.

Lord, help us to pray for people who do wicked things.

Have I ever been bitten or stung by anything?

THURS

In the spring, at the time when kings go off to war ... (1 Chron. 20:1)

When King David was alive, spring was the time for the battles to begin – not a lot for the soldiers and their families to look forward to throughout the winter months. Thankfully, today it is different. I love spring. I am not a great lover of the long dark nights and I do enjoy seeing more daylight, warmer weather, the flowers beginning to grow and the leaves forming on the trees. It seems like new life is beginning. With Easter also in spring it is also great to be reminded of Jesus dying and rising again from the dead and giving you and me the opportunity to start a brand new life, living for Him.

Lord, thank You for spring, and thank You for the new life that You have given to us.

Which is my favourite season?

FRI

"Where, O death, is your victory? Where, O death, is your sting?" (1 Cor. 15:55)

We have all seen a long black car called a hearse go slowly past us. If we look in the window we will see men dressed in black and looking very sad. In the back of the hearse is a wooden box containing the one who has died; sometimes it is covered in flowers and cards. The car behind is even sadder. Inside it are the relatives of the one who has died. Death is always sad, and to lose a loved one is like a terrible painful sting. But it's not all bad news. When someone who loves Jesus dies, they go and live with Him forever. Death is the Christian's door into heaven where there will be no more pain and no more sadness.

Lord, thank You that the grave is not the end, it's just the beginning.

Am I scared of death?

SAT

"Enlarge the place of your tent, stretch your tent curtains wide, do not hold back." (Isa. 54:2)

Here we see Isaiah prophesying that good times would come in the future and he uses the picture of the tent to express this. Most of us have been camping. When our children were smaller we would go every year, it was really the only holiday that we could afford and it was always a lot of fun. When we think about it, though, a tent only takes up a tiny space. Five of us would eat and sleep in an area not much bigger than our car. God promises us great things if we follow Him, so we had better get ready to expand our tent area for all the good things that He has in store for us.

Lord, help us to be ready for all the great things You have got lined up for us.

What sort of holidays do I enjoy the most?

Week 36

SUN

CD 2: 10

"There is no dark place ... where evildoers can hide." (Job 34:22)

In most films if someone is going to do some bad deed, we usually find them creeping around in the darkness of the night, or lurking in the shadows. They do not want to be in the light, they want to be hidden by darkness so no one can see what they are up to. Sometimes when we do wrong things, we think that God cannot see us, or doesn't know what we are thinking. God can see everything, however dark it is, that is why it is important that when we do wrong things we own up to them, and say sorry to Him and anyone we have hurt.

Lord, we know we can never keep a secret from You.

Should I keep secrets?

MON

No-one has ever seen God.
(1 John 4:12)

Have you ever met someone who has told you that they cannot believe in God because they cannot see Him and it's impossible to believe in something that you cannot see? I wonder if they believe in electricity? They cannot see it but every time they switch that switch on, they expect to see a light bulb light up. True, we cannot see God, but we can see a bit of Him in His wonderful creation. Look at the sea, the stars, the flowers, animals, birds and a new-born baby. As we look at His wonderful creation I would have thought that it is harder *not* to believe in God than it is to believe in Him.

Lord, we can't see You, but we can see Your beauty in the things You have created.

What else do I believe exists even though I can't see it with my eyes?

TUES

"... let the man of God ... teach us how to bring up the boy who is to be born." (Judg. 13:8)

Manoah was Samson's dad and he had been given specific instructions on how God wanted his child to be raised. Manoah, like most dads, wanted to get it right and wanted more help on how to do the job properly. Raising children in God's way is no easy task, as any children reading this may discover in a few years' time. I think that most of us parents do our best, but when we get stuck it is no shame to get advice from other godly parents who may be older than us and whose children have grown up. None of us have all the answers, that's why the family of God needs to listen to advice from others – even if in the end we may not take it.

Lord, help us to be able to advise, or to listen to advice, regarding children.

How would I feel if Samson were my son?

WEDS

"Thus the saying 'One sows and another reaps' is true." (John 4:37)

I love the work that God has called me to do. Although it is not always the easiest, I do praise God for it. Every week I am singing songs and sharing the good news of Jesus with men, women, boys and girls throughout the world and nearly every week I see people deciding to give their lives to Jesus. That's the joy of being a reaper. I also know that for years before I arrive on the scene, parents, children's workers, friends etc. have been doing all the hard work – week in week out sowing the Word of God into lives. I could not be a reaper without the faithful sowers, and I praise God for them.

Lord, thank You for both the sowers and the reapers.

Am I a sower or a reaper?

THURS

A woman should learn in quietness and full submission. (1 Tim. 2:11)

Without entering the "what women should and should not do" debate I think we Christians have to be very careful that we do not teach one thing to children when they are young, then change it when they get older. For instance, how many children's meetings teach that little girls should learn in silence while the boys are encouraged to contribute? At all the meetings I am involved in I encourage all my little listeners to contribute and join in. We must be very careful if we say this to our little girls when they are young, but then tell them they need to be silent when they get older. We could quite rightly face the accusation of leading them into confusion.

Lord, help us not to confuse children.

Should girls be quiet while boys can speak?

FRI

"She will give birth to a son, and you are to give him the name Jesus ..." (Matt. 1:21)

Joseph was a good man and probably quite a lot older than Mary. They had been dating for some time, all was going well and then suddenly he discovered that she was going to have a baby, and it certainly was not his. One night as he slept an angel appeared to him in a dream telling him not to worry as God was the Father, and that he should call the baby Jesus because He would save the people from their sins. When Joseph woke up he did all that the angel had said. Joseph really must have been a very obedient man, which I guess is why God chose him.

Lord, help us to be obedient and do the things You ask us to do.

How would I have coped if I had been Joseph?

SAT

I was pushed back and about to fall, but the Lord helped me. (Psa. 118:13)

I remember once being a little bored at a Christian conference, so a friend and I crept out into the garden to have some fun. There was a long low wall and we decided to play a game of trying to push each other off the wall by just using our shoulders. My friend was a bit bigger than I was and I ended up flying off the wall and cracking my ribs! We have all at times been pushed off the wall spiritually, all it takes is someone to say an unkind word to us or put us down. Let's never forget that we may often be pushed, but the Lord is always there to help us to stand straight back up again.

Lord, help us to realise that every time we are unfairly pushed, You are always right behind to stabilise us.

What is the worst fall that I have ever had?

SUN

CD 2: 11

Delight yourself in the Lord and he will give you the desires of your heart. (Psa. 37:4)

Sometimes we think that God only wants us to do things that we will find hard or things that we will not want to do. When I was 14 I was in a rock band and really enjoyed making music. At that age I had no idea that nearly 40 years later I would be performing at concerts, working for many weeks of the year in a recording studio and producing and arranging songs. God often gives us, and allows us to develop, the desires of our hearts, which believe it or not are the things we enjoy doing. But let's not forget that first we must take delight in the Lord, which means being totally dependent upon Him.

Lord, we depend on You, please give us the desires of our hearts.

What do I most desire?

MON

I can do everything through him who gives me strength. (Phil. 4:13)

This verse by itself sounds great, but it follows on from Paul explaining that he had known what it's like to be in need, and he'd known what it's like to have plenty. He'd also known what it's like to be both well fed and hungry. This means that there may be times when we are hungry and in need, but that's not always a sign that we are out of the will of God. Then, continues Paul, when we are content in all situations nothing will be impossible for us to do in God's strength. So that's all we need to do. Be as happy and contented when we are hungry or in need as we are when we are well fed and have plenty. Hmmm, that's the hard one!

Lord, help us to be content whether we have plenty or very little.

At this moment, am I content with what I have?

TUES

So Lot chose for himself the whole plain of Jordan and set out towards the east. (Gen. 13:11)

Travelling together was not working for good friends Abraham and his nephew, Lot. There was just not enough grass for their massive flocks and herds. Abraham did not want to lose his friendship with Lot, so he gave him first choice of the land. Lot saw the best land was towards the east and chose that. The problem was, while Lot chose what looked good, he also chose to head towards Sodom and Gomorrah which were two of the most wicked places on earth. What's best is not always what looks good. Best is learning to choose what God wants us to have.

Lord, help us to know the difference between what looks good to us, and what's best to You.

Let me tell you about the nicest place that I have been to.

WEDS

... neither death nor life ... will be able to separate us from the love of God ... (Rom. 8:38-39)

But it's not just "death nor life", the verse continues, it's "neither angels nor demons, neither the present nor the future, nor any powers, neither height nor depth, nor anything else in all creation". I think that just about covers everything. We must never forget this Bible verse when we are feeling all alone and thinking that nobody cares for us or loves us. Nothing and no one can ever separate us from God's love. You'd think that the whole world would want to become Christians just by reading this verse wouldn't you.

Lord, thank You that nothing could stop You loving us.

When I am feeling lonely, would I consider looking at my Bible?

THURS

When times are good, be happy ... when ... bad, consider: God has made the one as well as the other. (Eccl. 7:14)

I love holidays, especially if we manage to go somewhere hot. For weeks before, I am thinking about it, buying all the essential books and getting very excited. One year when we went to Spain the sun was shining and the sea was blue and I was very happy – until we arrived at our hotel. It was terrible. We were on a building site, surrounded by damp peeling walls, and we saw little creatures running all over the floor. After all my excitement, I was very disappointed and had a really bad time. But I believe we need both good and bad times because the bad times make the good times seem even better. Our next holiday was fantastic!

Lord, thank You for both the good and the bad times.

What is the worst holiday I have ever had?

FRI

I will sing of the Lord's great love for ever. (Psa. 89:1)

One thing I was never blessed with was a brilliant voice and I guess it's God's little joke that over the years, I have released more than 30 albums with me singing on them. My voice may not be the most tuneful, but it is sincere! I have learned that God does not just enjoy *good* singing, He seems to enjoy all singing, especially if a person is singing their praises to Him. Now I am not saying that all us croakers should rush and grab a microphone but I am saying when we are by ourselves let's have a good old sing about the Lord's love, He seems to enjoy a joyful noise as much as a tuneful one.

Lord, we want to always sing about Your wonderful love.

Would I ever dare go to the front at a church meeting and sing a solo?

SAT

Let heaven and earth praise him, the seas and all that move in them.

(Psa. 69:34)

The highest heavens, the lowest earth, even the rolling sea and all the thousands of creatures that live in it were made to praise God. Often we think that it is just we humans who know how to praise. I guess that we are the only part of creation that can choose to praise the Lord or choose not to. I believe when we choose to praise Him it excites the Lord more than any other thing or creature possibly could. It's so sad that while all creation is praising God, many people choose not to and miss out on one of the greatest experiences that we can have while we are on earth.

Lord, thank You that all creation including us can enjoy praising You.

What creature do I find hardest to imagine praising God?

Week 38

SUN

CD 2: 12

People were bringing little children to Jesus ... but the disciples rebuked them ...

(Mark 10:13–16)

We must not think too badly of the disciples for presuming that Jesus only had time for adults, many Christians still think that today. In most of our churches the adults are treated as more important and get superior venues, musicians, equipment, teachers and, of course, budgets. Some parents sometimes consider their little ones a "distraction" to their personal worship and like the disciples are happy to push their children into another room out of their way. Jesus loves blessing children. Where you find children, you will find Jesus – you will also find me!

Lord, thank You that You always have time for the little ones.

Do I prefer to be with or without children in church meetings?

MON

Shall I come to you with a whip, or in love and with a gentle spirit?

(1 Cor. 4:21)

I never really much liked circuses. I always felt that somewhere down the line, someone must have been cruel to these poor animals to make them do such crazy tricks, so much against their nature. I remember seeing the lions looking far more scared than their tamer, which is not surprising as he spent most of the time cracking a ferocious long whip at them. Paul brought correction to those who needed it by being loving and gentle, not through fear. In our families and in our churches we must do the same.

Lord, help us to be loving and gentle if we need to correct anyone.

What do I think is cruel?

TUES

Dear friends, let us love one another, for love comes from God.

(1 John 4:7)

I remember once leading a team at a Bible camp, and someone, who was new to the team, was under pressure and completely lost it. This person started putting me down in front of all the team and told me how useless I was as leader. I felt like bursting into tears. Later that day, I prayed with this person, and we hugged each other, and to this day we have been good friends. We must love each other, even after hurtful things have been said, because love comes from God, and we belong to Him.

Lord, because love comes from You, we must love others.

Are there people that I find it impossible to love?

WEDS "For I knew how stubborn you were ..." (Isa. 48:4)

A close friend of mine is sometimes criticised for not being very good at making decisions. When hearing two people discussing opposite viewpoints and asked his opinion, he usually says that he can see both sides of the argument and agrees with both. I remember once he did make a decision, which on reflection was a wrong one, but he stubbornly stuck to it just so that no one could accuse him of changing his mind. We must never be stubborn, that means immovable, and we must all be a little flexible even if we have strong opinions.

Lord, help us never to be stubborn.

When was I last stubborn?

THURS "Nazareth! Can anything good come from there?" Nathanael asked. (John 1:46)

Nazareth was a small insignificant town and not really famous for anything. Unlike Jerusalem and other cities and towns it does not even get a mention in the Old Testament. Nathanael was surprised that anyone important could come from such an unimportant place, yet he wonderfully changed his mind a few verses later, and recognised Jesus as the Son of God. It does not matter if we were born in a little village, an unknown town or a famous city, we are all important to God and He wants us to share the good news of Jesus with all our friends everywhere.

Lord, thank You for making us important, not insignificant.

Where would I most like to have been born.

FRI

"Praise and glory ... and honour and power and strength be to our God for ever and ever." (Rev. 7:12)

The angels were standing around the throne, then they fell down on their faces before the throne and worshipped. I wonder how much we really worship God, and I am not talking about singing songs. If the angels cannot stay upright when in the presence of Jesus how can we stay standing up or seated on a chair? I think if we really were in His presence, like the angels, we could not help but fall down on our faces before Him.

Lord, help us to be true worshippers.

Would I feel silly lying down on the floor in prayer?

SAT

I will lie down and sleep in peace, for you alone, O Lord, make me dwell in safety. (Psa. 4:8)

As a child I often had bad dreams. I had no idea what brought them about as I had not been watching unhelpful things on the television or reading books that could have brought on these nightmares. I wanted to sleep with my door open and my light on and I was frightened to close my eyes. My parents prayed for me, and in time I was able to put my head on the pillow knowing that God was protecting me at night, as well as in the daytime. I think at the end of a day when so much has passed through the mind, both young and old need to realise that God wants us to sleep well and feel protected.

Lord, thank You for protecting us while we are asleep.

When did I last have a bad dream?

SUN

CD 2: 13

"... but if you do not forgive men their sins, your Father will not forgive your sins." (Matt. 6:14–15)

I was speaking at a conference a few years ago and felt all was going well, everyone seemed to be enjoying what I was saying. However, a week after I returned home I received a very critical letter from a person who had attended, which was totally negative and very upsetting. I wrote back saying that I was disappointed that this person had not come and shared these views with me while I was there and that I would not carry on arguing in a letter, goodbye. Nothing happened for a year, then I felt the Lord telling me to write back and send greetings, which I did and had a lovely letter in return. We must not only forgive people, we must also try and put things right with them.

Lord help us to not only forgive, but to go out of our way to try and make things right.

Is there someone I should be putting things right with?

MON

And they cried out ... "Salvation belongs to our God ... and to the Lamb." (Rev. 7:10)

I remember once, when our boys were small, we were climbing up Mount Snowdon when the weather suddenly turned very bad. At one stage little Daniel started to slip down over a steep edge and I grabbed his hand just in time to save him from falling down the mountain. Although I may have saved Daniel from getting hurt, Jesus has saved us from losing our lives forever. Although He is our best friend, He is also the King of kings who sits on a throne in heaven and the perfect Lamb of God who died on a cross so that we could really be saved. The book of Revelation will never let us forget how holy and powerful our best friend really is.

Lord, thank You for saving us.

Has anyone ever saved me from getting badly hurt?

TUES

"This is a remote place," they said, "and it's already very late. Send the people away ..." (Mark 6:35–36)

Here we see more than 5,000 people stuck in the middle of nowhere. They were keen to listen to Jesus but seemed to have lost all track of time. The disciples suggested that Jesus should do the sensible thing and dismiss them all before it got too late, after all everyone was getting hungry, and they had no food. Jesus, though, thought the sensible thing was to let them stay, and He then fed them all by using five loaves and a couple of fish. I wonder if some of the "sensible" people did leave early and miss one of the greatest miracles that has ever taken place. Perhaps we should not leave too quickly at the end of meetings ...

Lord, where Your power is present, that is where we want to be.

Have I ever left anywhere early, and afterwards wished I had stayed longer?

WEDS

Having nothing to do with godless myths and old wives' tales; rather, train yourself to be godly. (1 Tim. 4:7)

In the Early Church, a lot of myths and untrue stories were being taught that were built on Old Testament history and these were confusing people. Today we have our own myths about King Arthur, Robin Hood, fairies, and even Father Christmas. Although these myths are not necessarily dangerous, we must be aware that they can confuse: some children consider that fairies are angels, others think Father Christmas is the same as Father God. Personally, I think it's much wiser to teach the children truth, and nothing is truer than the most exciting book in the world, the Bible.

Help us teach what's true and want to learn what's right.

Should I teach others myths?

THURS

We remember the fish we ate in Egypt ... also the cucumbers, melons, leeks, onions and garlic. (Num. 11:5)

The Israelites started wailing to Moses, "We want meat to eat. We are fed up with the manna that the Lord is providing, when we were back in Egypt we ate ... " and our Scripture reading gives the list. These people were so ungrateful. They had forgotten all about the terrible way they had been treated as slaves and just thought of the good food they'd had. Memories are strange things. I have been in leadership in quite a few churches, and when things are difficult where I am now, I often think back to the blessings of the old days, rarely remembering the pressures and difficult times. It does not help to dwell on the past, today is the day the Lord has made, and I am grateful for it.

Lord, thank You for today and for all the good times.

In someone else's home, would I eat the food they had prepared for me even if I did not like it?

FRI

... when you lie down you will not be afraid ... your sleep will be sweet. (Prov. 3:24)

A while ago I visited Finland and stayed in a really nice hotel. In the middle of the night the drunken people in the next bedroom starting smashing up the room and even threw the television and chairs out of the window. It was not nice. I really felt a presence of evil and fear and could not get to sleep. After a while I cried out to the Lord and asked Him to put my mind at peace and help me to sleep, which of course He did. There will be times when we lie down that we may be frightened for all sorts of reasons. My advice is to talk to Jesus when this happens as He wants all His children's sleep to be sweet.

Lord, please help us to sleep soundly.

Have I ever been frightened by what I have heard while I have been in my bedroom?

SAT

"Be careful not to do your 'acts of righteousness' before men, to be seen by them." (Matt. 6:1)

A short while ago I saw someone who was homeless sitting by the side of the road. It was only a couple of days until Christmas and freezing cold and I felt really sorry for this person. I had coins in one pocket and a crisp £20 note in the other. I knew I should give the note so I walked over and as discreetly as I could, handed the money to the very appreciative person. Then came the temptation to tell someone about what I had just done so they could see what a nice generous guy I was. We must always be doing acts of kindness, but not to show how good we are, rather that we care for those who are less fortunate than we are.

Lord, help us not to have the wrong motives when we show people kindness.

How do I show kindness to those who are homeless?

Week 40

SUN

CD 2: 14

If God is for us, who can be against us? (Rom. 8:31)

It's so easy in this day and age to feel like an absolute loser. So often things do not seem to work out and we feel hopeless and useless. That's why we need always to remember today's reading. The evil one wants us to feel like losers and be down and miserable but our reading tells us that God is for us, supporting us, encouraging us, telling us that because of Jesus we are winners and we are victorious. If you are feeling a bit of a loser today, repeat this verse a few times. Almighty God who created the whole universe is on our side – and no enemy of His has a hope of ever being victorious.

Lord, thank You for making us winners.

When did I last feel like a loser?

MON

You have wearied the Lord with your words. (Mal. 2:17)

Many years ago I was in a van going to a booking with a very heavy, theatrical rock band. These guys were all good friends from Manchester and, as usual, I was doing all the talking. After a while the driver looked at me and said in a loud voice, "Will you shut up, your talking is driving me crazy." These north country folk always say it as it is! I wonder if the Lord ever gets fed up and weary with our words, especially when we do not mean what we are saying to Him. There is a time to speak and a time when our talk becomes tiresome both to God and other people, so we must know when to stop.

Lord help us to know when to stop talking.

What "drives me crazy"?

TUES

Be merciful to those who doubt. (Jude v.22)

Remember the disciple Thomas. After Jesus had been crucified, some of Thomas's friends told him that they had seen Jesus and that He was no longer dead – He was alive – but poor Thomas was full of doubts. "Unless I touch him myself, I will never believe," he said. Then Jesus appeared to him. Thomas never did actually need to touch Jesus, once he saw Him that was enough to take all his doubts away. It's great that Thomas was still one of Jesus' best friends, even with all his doubts.

Lord help us not to have any doubts about You being alive today.

What do I find is the hardest thing in the Bible to believe?

WEDS A fool finds no pleasure in understanding but delights in airing his own opinions. (Prov. 18:2)

When I was at Bible College, I was quite a young Christian and felt rather unqualified to join in with some of the "heated" theological debates. What I found strange was that sometimes an elderly lecturer, who had spent a lifetime studying a subject was set upon by a young student who quite honestly did not know what he was talking about. Even after the lecturer had tried to explain the point again, the young student would have none of it and left the lecture feeling good with himself that he had put over his point of view. A foolish person who just likes the sound of his own voice and refuses to listen to those who are more experienced will never understand anything.

Lord, help me not just to agree with me!

Who do I most like airing my opinions to?

THURS "Look! I see four men walking around in the fire, unbound and unharmed ..." (Dan. 3:25)

It's great to watch fire burning, but we must never forget how dangerous it can be. Every year we read of uncontrollable fires destroying thousands of acres of land, and everything that gets in its path. Shadrach, Meshach and Abednego worshipped God and refused to bow down to the idol that the king had made so they were thrown into a blazing furnace. Being obedient to God meant that they were not only unharmed by the fire, they were also joined by a heavenly being, possibly an angel. If people ask us to do wrong things, we must say no. Whatever the outcome God will be with us.

Lord, help us to be brave and stay obedient to You.

What do I like and dislike about heat and fire?

FRI

Dear friend, do not imitate what is evil but what is good. (3 John v.11)

I used to love watching the children of one of our leaders during the meetings. The little girl was a few years older than her brother and wherever she walked, he walked, whenever she danced he danced, he would copy everything that his older sister did. The problem came when she did something that was naughty, because of course little brother did the naughty thing as well. It is good to copy the good things that people do, but we must remember that these people are human, and are going to do wrong things as well. Let's not imitate the bad things that people do, however exciting it may look.

Lord, help us not to copy bad things that people do.

What good and bad things that I see my friends doing do I copy?

SAT

The Lord will be king over the whole earth. (Zech 14:9)

The Roman Empire covered a lot of the world and the Caesars were kings over massive empires. The problem was they never seemed to reign for long. In just over 80 years there were eleven Caesars which proves the point. Christians believe that one day Jesus, the King of kings, is going to come back and rule the earth. This will be the end of Satan and everything bad, and the great news is that Jesus will rule and reign forever.

Lord, thank You for being the King who will reign forever.

What do I think of royalty today?

SUN

CD 2: 15

Set a guard over my mouth, O Lord. (Psa. 141:3)

I am not in any way a violent person, in fact I do not like even watching boxing and still feel shocked if I see anyone fighting in the street. I would find it hard to lash out and hit anyone. But at times I can still be very aggressive, not with my fists, but with my lips. Sometimes I open my mouth and really hurt people by what I say. We can damage people for life through words. I must ask the Lord to help me guard my mouth and what I say. I want to bless people with my speech not destroy them by foolish and potentially dangerous words.

Lord, please help us to think before we speak.

Can I think of any times when I may have hurt people by the things I have said?

MON

So I will always remind you of these things, even though you know them ... (2 Pet. 1:12)

I remember once when I was pastor of a local church, teaching at a Bible study and at the end of the evening wondering how much of what I had said would be remembered by my listeners. A while later a friend of mine came and gave practically the same talk to the same people and some of them commented on how wonderfully fresh the talk had been, they could not remember hearing anything like that before! We all need to be reminded of God's truths time and time again. Even though we think we know them, we soon tend to forget to live them out.

Lord, thank You for those who keep reminding us of Your teaching.

When was the last time I forgot to do something?

TUES "These people say, 'The time has not yet come for the Lord's house to be built.'" (Hag. 1:2)

Here we find God's people living in luxury and having fun, while making excuses why it was not the right time to start rebuilding God's house. The prophet Haggai's job was to tell them to get on their feet and get building if they wanted to please God. We are often like them. There are things that God wants us to do but we tell Him that we will do them a little later, and we make all sorts of excuses why we can't right now. When God says He wants something done, I think He means He wants it done right away.

Lord, help us to obey You immediately and not make up excuses why we can't.

When did I last make up an excuse for not doing something that needed doing?

WEDS "But they will never follow a stranger." (John 10:5)

Jesus said that His sheep would run away from a stranger because they do not recognise His voice. Many a time I have been invited into the homes of people who own big aggressive-looking dogs. They walk into their house shouting at the dog to stop barking then, as they hold the dog's collar, they invite me in, assuring me that their canine monster would not dream of hurting me. I am never convinced that they are telling me the truth, because the dogs may recognise their master's voice, but they certainly would not recognise mine. We know what the voice of the Good Shepherd sounds like so let's run away from any other voice that may wish to lead us away from Him.

Lord, help us to always follow You and nobody else.

What dogs do I like best?

THURS

But Jonah ran away from the Lord and headed for Tarshish. (Jonah 1:3)

Jonah probably had many reasons for not wanting to obey God and go to Nineveh but none of them were right. We all know the story well – into the boat, into the storm, into the sea, into the big fish, then onto the beach and finally on to Nineveh. A sort of scary, smelly, horrible roundabout route to take, really. We can never run away from God so when He tells us to do something let's not try and do the opposite, there are still a lot of big fishes out there.

Lord, help us never to think that we can run away from You.

Imagine what it would be like to live inside a fish for three days.

FRI

"Nineveh has more than [120,000] people ... Should I not be concerned about that great city?" (Jonah 4:11)

Poor Jonah. After his voyage in the big fish he at last told the people of Nineveh about their forthcoming destruction. However, surprise surprise, they were all very sorry, so God forgave them. Jonah was miserable that they had not been destroyed and sat under a large vine to shade himself from the hot sun. Then when his vine died, Jonah was very angry, he actually felt more compassion for the departed vine than he did for all the people that lived in Nineveh. I guess he learned his lesson in the end. It is wonderful the way God reasoned with Jonah, and never gave up on him.

Lord, thank You for being so patient with us.

Are there times when I feel more sorry for animals than people?

SAT

Finally, brothers, pray for us ...

(2 Thess. 3:1)

I remember being at a conference once and late one night one of the speakers approached me as he was heading for bed and told me that he felt quite unwell. He was very grateful when I told him that I would pray for him that night. But I forgot to. The following morning one of the delegates who had just been to this man's session told me that he had announced at the front how well he was feeling and that it was due to Ishmael's prayer – I felt terrible. Whenever we tell people that we will remember them in prayer, we MUST remember to pray for them.

Lord, help us to keep our word.

Can I remember a time when I said I would pray for someone, and then forgot all about it?

Week 42

SUN

CD 2: 16

I am not ashamed of the gospel ...

(Rom. 1:16)

Throughout our married life, there have been times when Irene has been both ashamed and embarrassed by my crazy behaviour. I remember once when we were in a large supermarket, I went to the information desk and asked them to find Irene for me. Soon everyone heard: "Could Irene Smale please come to the information desk" and poor Irene arrived red-faced and there I was, giggling. I know it was a naughty thing to do and Irene had every right to be ashamed of me. Jesus never did anything wrong, so we should never be ashamed to tell anyone about Him. In fact we should be so proud that we have such a wonderful Friend and Saviour, we should want to tell everyone about Him.

Lord, help us never to be ashamed about passing on the good news of Jesus.

When was the last time someone embarrassed me?

MON

... David sent Joab out ... But David remained in Jerusalem. (2 Sam. 11:1)

Many a time on my travels I have arrived in the right town but walked into the wrong church building, surprising those inside when I have asked where the Ishmael meeting is. King David should have led his men to battle, but he chose to be in the wrong place at the wrong time. There are certain places where God would want us to be and specific times when He wants us to be there, let's live our lives by His timetable and not just ours.

Lord, help us to be in the right place at the right time.

Have I ever found myself in the wrong place by accident?

TUES

From the roof he saw a woman bathing. (2 Sam. 11:2)

David is not on the battlefield where he should have been. But things have got worse, David was not only in the wrong place, he was also on his roof looking at things that he should not have been looking at. Of course there is nothing sinful about the human body because it is beautifully made by God, but since Adam and Eve sinned, we cover it up because sometimes people can think wrong things when they see nakedness. Sadly, David was one of those people who did think wrong things and then also did some very bad things. If only he had been on the battlefield with his men all this might never have happened.

Lord, help us not to look at things that may lead us into sin.

Can I think of something that I have seen or watched that I now wish I hadn't?

WEDS

The Pharisees ... began to oppose him ... waiting to catch him in something he might say. (Luke 11:53–54)

I have had one or two people in my meetings over the years who are not really interested in what I have to say, they are only listening to see if I say something that they can object to. These sort of people are quite dangerous. The Pharisees were like this with Jesus, but there are two big differences. The first is that I do say wrong things, Jesus never did, and the second is, the people who oppose me are just wanting to argue with me but the people who were opposing Jesus were wanting to find a reason to kill Him.

Lord, help us never to be deliberately argumentative.

Who do I most enjoy listening to as they teach me about Jesus?

THURS

The Sovereign Lord is my strength. (Hab. 3:19)

The word "sovereign" is a very old word. It was first used in France in the thirteenth century and as it has the word "reign" at the end of it, we tend to think of kings and queens who reign over us. Nowadays kings and queens have very little power and the most important person in most nations is the president or the prime minister. When the Lord is called Sovereign we see the real meaning of the word. The Sovereign Lord in our reading means that God is the one with supreme authority and there is no other living person who this could apply to.

Thank You, Lord, that no one could ever be as important and as powerful as You.

What would I most like to ask the royal family, prime minister or president?

FRI

His sister asked ... "Shall I go and get one of the Hebrew women to nurse the baby for you?" (Exod. 2:7)

This is a wonderful story. Moses' mum thought she had saved her child from death by the wicked Pharaoh, but then she could so easily have lost him forever to Pharaoh's daughter. However, thanks to the quick thinking of her own daughter she ends up being paid to raise her own son. We must also remember that the word "nurse" is not just a childminder. Little Moses needed to be fed milk, and it's great to see again that it would be his mum who would be holding him close and feeding him through those very important early years.

Lord, help us to be able to think quickly and give wise answers when we need to.

What would make me want to be a nurse – or not want to?

SAT

"I will pour out my Spirit on all people." (Joel 2:28)

I love this verse; in the rest of it we read that sons and daughters will prophesy, old men will dream dreams and young men will see visions. In other words, all ages will be filled with the Holy Spirit and used by God. I still find people who think children cannot be Spirit-filled – they must be people who have not read this scripture. I have had the privilege to pray for all ages to be filled with the Holy Spirit and when our verse says ALL people, I guarantee it means ALL people!

Lord, please keep filling us with Your Holy Spirit.

How can I tell if someone has been "filled with the Holy Spirit"?

SUN

CD 2: 17

So, if you think you are standing firm, be careful that you don't fall.

(1 Cor. 10:12)

There are times when I have felt great, really close to God and convinced that nothing was ever going to make me sin and do wrong things again. It's usually when I am feeling this good that I am tempted with different sins, maybe pride or maybe bad thoughts – and sure enough I often give in to them, and instead of standing firm I fall. We must try and stand firm in God, but let's always be aware that when we do, it is the most likely time that the evil one will come around to try and knock us down.

Lord, please help us to stand firm and not to fall.

When was the last time I felt really good?

MON

He showed them his hands and side.

(John 20:20)

How did Jesus' bodily appearance change after Golgotha (otherwise known as "skull hill")? Before Golgotha Jesus' body was perfect but at Golgotha He had blunt nails banged into His hands and His feet as He was hung up on a wooden cross. Later a spear was pushed into His side to make sure that He was really dead. After Golgotha Jesus showed His friends His wounds to prove to them that He was no longer dead, but alive. Today, we remember Jesus' wounds when we take communion, where we also celebrate that He is alive today.

Lord, help us never to forget the pain You went through so that our sins can be forgiven.

Should all believers, whatever age, be able to take part in communion?

TUES The disciples were overjoyed when they saw the Lord. (John 20:20)

This of course comes as no surprise. They had the three very best years of their lives walking around with their best friend Jesus, and then He was crucified and died. We can never know the depression and confusion that the disciples must have felt in that short period between the crucifixion and the resurrection. Now we read that Jesus is back with them again and I think the word "overjoyed" must be a massive understatement. We should be very grateful that we have never had to go through that sort of confusion and depression. Ever since we have been born Jesus has been alive, and He is never going to die again.

Thank You, Lord, for being alive today.

What makes me feel depressed?

WEDS The Lord is slow to anger and great in power. (Nahum 1:3)

A lot of my life is spent in my car. For more than 30 years I have driven all over Britain speaking and singing at various events, and usually Irene is my trusty map reader sitting in the passenger seat next to me. Not many things get me angry but I do find I start to boil over if she has got us lost. Once I upset her so much she nearly threw the map out of the window. Our verse today tell us that although the Lord does get angry, it is a controlled anger and only over important issues. We must try not to get angry over silly things.

Lord, help us to control our anger.

When was the last time I got angry?

THURS Marriage should be honoured by all ... (Heb. 13:4)

Due to a very full diary, it was only a 12-week period between my first date with Irene, and walking up the aisle to say "I do". But we did know that being together was part of God's plan for both our lives. Nowadays many people think that marriage is not important and it's fine to just live together and bring up a family. The Bible, however, says that marriage is very special. It is not just a church service, signing a form or exchanging rings, it is something that God wants loving couples to do and to take very seriously.

Lord, we pray for any who may be experiencing difficulties in their marriages.

What friends do I know who I think have happy marriages?

FRI "Consecrate yourselves, for tomorrow the Lord will do amazing things among you." (Josh. 3:5)

"Consecrate" means to make holy – in this case it meant the people needed to get things right with God. When they had sorted their lives out God was going to supernaturally dry up the River Jordan so they could cross over it on dry land, and then of course miraculously provide a way for them to conquer the fortress of Jericho. I wonder if sometimes we do not see the wonderful miracles that God has lined up for us because we are not holy, and have not put things right with Him.

Lord please help us to be holy.

Do you think that God does not do certain things for us because we have not got things right with Him?

SAT

But avoid foolish controversies and genealogies and arguments and quarrels ... (Titus 3:9)

"Genealogies" is a long word but it simply means someone's family tree or their ancestors. Here Paul is writing a personal letter to his friend Titus. Paul is encouraging Titus to try and stop the people from this church on the island of Crete arguing about unimportant things of the past and present. Remember, talking and debating is not wrong, it is a way of learning and went on a lot in the Bible and still goes on a lot with Christians of all ages today. However, if we are going to spend time discussing subjects and issues, let's make sure that they are relevant and important and we are not just wasting time.

Lord, help us not to get involved in foolish discussions.

What subjects is it good to discuss?

Week 44

SUN

CD 2: 18

"Don't be afraid ... Those who are with us are more than those who are with them." (2 Kings 6:16)

Many years ago I was invited to sing a few songs in an army barracks bar. As I got on stage I was quite scared as most of my listeners were drunk and some looked very aggressive. It was one of those situations where I had to believe that God's angels were surrounding me, and were much stronger than the army boys I was facing. It was a good time, although in the last song one person had drunk so much that he fell unconscious on the stage just missing me. At times we may feel afraid, but let's never forget the angels God sends to protect us.

Lord, thank You for angels.

What are the differences between us and angels?

MON

Do not be like the horse or the mule, which have no understanding ... (Psa. 32:9)

I used to love horse riding. Every Saturday I would be at the stables and if I helped clean them out I would get a free ride. The trouble was some of these horses were so strong and stubborn that even pulling on their reins and with the bit in their mouths, it took a lot of strength to steer them in the right direction. God does not want to have to control us like a horse. He will not use reins and a bridle to steer us in the right direction, He wants us to *choose* to be obedient and follow Him.

“” **Lord, thank You for not forcing us to do things but allowing us choice.**

? **What do I like and not like about horses?**

TUES

When you ask, you do not receive, because you ask with wrong motives. (James 4:3)

I have never been very rich, but often I think that I would like to be. I sometimes think I should pray about winning a lot of money and then all my worries would be over. I could travel around the world telling people about Jesus and never have to charge any money for any of my concerts. I could even afford to give away all my CDs instead of selling them. Then I could buy a better house and a better car, good clothes and have some wonderful holidays. However, I do not think I will ever be very rich because God knows that even with all my wonderful intentions I would end up spending a lot of that money on *me*.

“” **Lord, please help us to ask You for things with the right motives.**

? **How would I spend a million pounds?**

WEDS

You should not look down on your brother in the day of his misfortune. (Obad. 1:12)

There is a well-known expression about kicking a man when he is down. In other words, although we can see someone is going through a difficult time, we still have a go at them. Let's remember, we are all going to have bad days when we need encouraging not discouraging. When someone is going through hard times let's not look down on them, let's try and lift them up, then maybe they will do the same for us when we next reach a low spot in our lives.

Lord, help us to be an encouragement to anyone who is having a bad day.

When did I last have a bad day?

THURS

"Ask and it will be given to you." (Matt. 7:7)

I remember a saying, "Those who ask won't get". I also remember another saying, "Those who don't ask, don't want". You just can't win with some people can you. Jesus makes His feelings very clear, if we ask He will give, if we don't ask, we could miss out. Of course this does not mean that He will give us everything that we ask for, but He will give us everything that He wants us to have.

Lord, help us not to be frightened to ask You for things.

Discussion point. What would I like to ask Jesus for today?

FRI "Seek and you will find." (Matt. 7:7)

I am known for losing things. I lose my keys – I put them down somewhere and forget where I've put them; my wallet – it's in a pocket somewhere; even my wife – I know I have arranged to meet her somewhere – but where? Whether we lose things or whether we don't, all the best things have to be sought after. The Bible is full of hidden treasures but you have to search to find them, and life is full of excitement but we have to keep our eyes on the Lord Jesus if we want to find the best life possible. Life is full of seeking and finding.

Lord, we know the more we seek, the more we'll find.

Can I think of anything I have lost that has never been found?

SAT "Knock and the door will be opened to you." (Matt. 7:7)

When I was young, some nights in our village, we kids would get very bored. There really was nowhere to go and nothing to do. To relieve our boredom we would go up and down the road knocking on people's doors and then running away when they opened them. There will be a lot of doors in our lives that we should knock on, but let's keep on knocking till they open and not run away. On life's journey, we will find Jesus opening those doors for us, and behind those doors are all sorts of wonderful things that He has in store for those who follow Him. Never give up knocking.

Lord, help us never to give up knocking on doors which will lead us on to new adventures with You.

It was wrong to knock on doors and run away. Why?

SUN

CD 2: 19

"The least of you will become a thousand, the smallest a mighty nation." (Isa. 60:22)

Although our reading probably means that with God's help a small family can become a tribe and a tribe can become a mighty nation, it also reminds me of something else. Imagine, when Jesus walked on the earth, there were only 11 of His 12 disciples, plus a very few of His listeners, that could be classed as true followers and they all lived in Israel. From this tiny group, today, over 2,000 years later, we will find millions of followers of Jesus of all ages and they are in every country we can think of. A little baby once in a manger has now the greatest following the world has ever known.

Lord, it's great to be part of Your massive family.

Count up the number of living relatives you have.

MON

"Love your enemies ..." (Matt. 5:44)

In my book *Reclaiming a Generation* I wrote, "I have no real enemies, but I think I may have a few very close friends who don't like me much." It's true, I don't think I have any enemies, but I can think of a few people who I do not like much. These people have upset me at one time or another and it's easier to avoid them than to love them. Looking at our Scripture verse I think these are the people that Jesus does not want me to avoid, I think He wants me to go out of my way to show them that I love them. It's a hard one but if that's what Jesus wants, that's what I must do.

Lord, help us to love the people that we don't like much.

Who am I going to find it hardest to show love to?

TUES

Isaac ... loved Esau, but Rebekah loved Jacob. (Gen. 25:28)

Isaac and Rebekah may have loved God but they were not so good at loving their children. Both Jacob and Esau would have known that they were loved by one parent more than the other and that must have brought about all sorts of upsets and playing one against the other in the home. It is not surprising that the two brothers did not get on very well either. In family life there must be no favourites, every child is different and children need to be loved equally. If we fail to pass on this love while they are children, I do believe that it can affect them later on in adult life.

Lord, help us to show love to all our family.

Do I feel more loved by my mother, my father or both equally?

WEDS

They mourned and wept and fasted till evening for Saul and his son Jonathan ... (2 Sam. 1:12)

The king and the prince were both dead and David was heartbroken. Sooner or later we will all know what it is like to have someone we love die and we too will feel like David. If a Christian dies, some feel they should celebrate because the one who has died has gone to be with Jesus, but we must be real. It is right for those left on earth to have a time of mourning and weeping. It is also biblical, some of God's best friends mourned when loved ones died, even though they knew that one day they would see them again.

Help us not to be frightened to mourn or weep when a loved one dies.

Saul was not very nice to David, what did David like about Saul?

THURS

But Martha was distracted by all the preparations that had to be made. (Luke 10:40)

Irene and I were once invited to a friend's home for a meal. I remember suggesting we get a take-away so we could spend some time talking together but the wife insisted on cooking. By the end of the evening we had eaten a wonderful meal but had hardly spoken to the wife as she spent the evening in the kitchen. I do not think that Jesus was too worried about what Martha was going to cook, He just wanted to sit down and spend time with her and Mary. Food's OK, but fellowship is more important.

Lord, help us never to put preparation before people.

What is the greatest distraction when I am trying to talk to someone?

FRI

But the Lord provided a great fish to swallow Jonah ... (Jonah 1:17)

I guess as Jonah was thrown overboard into the rough sea, he must have thought "This is the end, it can't get worse I'm going to drown." Then he must have seen this monstrous fish with its mouth wide open heading towards him and he probably thought, "Perhaps things can get worse after all!" He would never have guessed that the big fish was sent by God to prevent him drowning and to be his transportation back to dry land. If we think things can't get worse, they probably can. But that may also be our route to better times.

Lord, please help us to see that bad times can lead to good times.

What would it be like being in a fish's stomach?

SAT

Dear friend, I pray that you may enjoy good health ... (3 John 2)

It always makes me smile when I see people toasting with a glass of whiskey and saying the words "Good health". I think not. Nowadays, however, people tend to have gone to the other extreme and become health fanatics. In the gym, in the swimming pool, jogging around the streets, even standing in front of the TV and imitating the movements of some slim mega-star. Trying to keep our bodies fit is fine, but only if we spend even more time keeping our spiritual life fit because at the end of the day, that is far more important.

“” **Lord, please keep us healthy in body and in spirit.**

? **How can I become more spiritually healthy?**

Week 46

SUN

CD 2: 20

... for all have sinned and fall short of the glory of God. (Rom. 3:23)

One of the meanings of the word *sin* is falling short of the mark. It was sometimes used of an archer when he shot his arrow at a target, if it did not reach that target it had sinned, fallen short of the mark. God's target for man that He created in His image was not to do wrong things and to be like Him. In the beginning Adam and Eve sinned and today you and I sin, we have all fallen short of God's perfect target. When we sin, let's be sure to say sorry to God.

“” **Lord, we are sorry that we so often fall short of how You want us to be.**

? **Do I think that God expects too much from me?**

MON

The king's heart is in the hand of the Lord. (Prov. 21:1)

A king in Solomon's day was a mighty ruler who often had the ultimate say in everything. However, although the king's heart may have been in the hands of the Lord, sadly many rulers never consult God before they make a decision. Nowadays many senior people in world government do not even believe in the existence of God, so it's not surprising that our world is in such a terrible state. Let's pray for those who govern our countries, let's pray they listen to God before they make decisions for the people they govern.

Lord, we pray that those who are in charge of our country will listen to You.

What decisions have governments made that we as Christians are not happy with?

TUES

"Are you really my son Esau?" Isaac asked. "I am," [Jacob] replied. (Gen. 27:24)

Isaac was very old and his eyesight had gone. He wanted to pray for both his sons before he died. In our reading we can see that Jacob wanted the first blessing, because that was always the best one and so he pretended to be his brother, Esau, who was the eldest, to get it. Then he even lied to his father. I sometimes hear people tell exaggerated stories of the miraculous to try and impress other Christians and to bless them. We should never deceive or lie but if we do, remember, we may fool people but we can never fool God.

Lord, help us never to deceive people.

What would I have felt and done if I had been Esau?

WEDS

Isaac asked him, "Who are you?" "I am your ... firstborn, Esau."

(Gen. 27:32)

In the days of our reading, a dying man's blessing was very important, he was passing on something special to his sons. Esau arrived back from hunting and, having prepared his dad's supper, discovered that Jacob had stolen the blessing that was meant for him – which once it had been said could not be taken back. Both old Isaac and Esau were devastated. The truth always comes out in the end and when people discover it, usually someone feels very hurt and the deceiver should feel very guilty.

Lord, if we have lied to anyone, please make us brave enough to own up and apologise to them.

What would I have felt and done if we had been Jacob?

THURS

"If you belonged to the world, it would love you as its own."

(John 15:19)

Some time ago, I went into a very small video shop to rent a film to watch for the evening. As I chose my film and went to pay for it I noticed the staff were all staring at a screen and watching a disgusting film that was probably illegal. I told them I was no longer interested in renting videos from them if this is what they were showing to the public, and walked out. I guess they thought me mad. They belong to this world and they love their own who enjoy what they enjoy. We Christians should have different standards which means that we will never really belong to this world we live in.

Lord, please help us not to love the wrong things that we see about us.

What makes Christians different from those who are not yet Christians?

FRI

Do not be overawed when a man grows rich, when the splendour of his house increases. (Psa. 49:16)

All around us are people who are earning, or borrowing, a lot of money to invest in their homes. Some are buying great big houses that they do not really need, while others are spending thousands improving houses that do not really need improving. It seems that if we have money we must spend it and homes are the obvious thing to spend it on. The next verse tells us that we cannot take our houses with us when we die. Let's pray before we spend; maybe as Christians we will think of better ways of investing our money that will benefit others not just ourselves.

Lord, please show us how we can best invest our money.

Who would I most like to give some money to if I had plenty?

SAT

"Therefore keep watch, because you do not know the day or the hour." (Matt. 25:13)

When someone was getting married in Bible times, the guests would only be told the date of the wedding, not the time. That would mean that they would need to be ready and waiting all day because the minute everything at the wedding ceremony was prepared, they would have to go immediately. The Lord Jesus is coming back one day for those who love Him, but no one knows the date or the time. Let's make sure that every day we are living a life that pleases Him, then when He does return, we will be ready to welcome Him.

Lord, help us always to be prepared for the wonderful day when You will return.

Are there any signs that Jesus may be back sooner rather than later?

SUN

CD 2: 21

The wicked man flees though no-one pursues, but the righteous are as bold as a lion. (Prov. 28:1)

Before Jacob died he spoke special words over his sons. He called Judah a lion's cub, which resembled royalty, strength and courage. Years later, the Lord Jesus was born into the family of Judah and in Revelation He is called the Lion of Judah. As Christians we too should be like lions. We are children of the King of kings, so we are royalty and we are bold because we have the power of the Holy Spirit living inside us. The wicked may run away, but as lions belonging to God, we have nothing to fear.

Lord, please make us as bold as lions.

What do I most admire about a lion?

MON

May your father and mother be glad; may she who gave you birth rejoice! (Prov. 23:25)

Quite a few of my teenage years were spent enjoying doing things that Christians should not enjoy doing. I always kept a friendship with my parents and would regularly visit them but as they were both committed Christians, throughout those years, I hardly gave them reason to be glad. I know now, though, that they never stopped praying for me, and in time God answered their prayers. I wonder how your mother and father feel or felt about you. We must always put God first, but our parents should have a special place in our lives.

Lord, help us to live a life that makes our parents glad that they brought us into this world.

What do I, or did I, do that would upset my parents?

TUES Turn my eyes away from worthless things. (Psa. 119:37)

It's strange how quickly our values change. Nowadays football seems to be one of the most important things in life, especially if you are a professional footballer. A while ago a famous footballer's little boy tragically died, and following this many footballers and commentators admitted that there are many things in life that are much more important and precious than football. People are far more valuable than any "things" but, sadly, for some it takes difficult or even tragic circumstances before they realise this.

Lord, help us to realise how precious people are.

As I look around what can I see that is precious or worthless?

WEDS Therefore encourage one another and build each other up ... (1 Thess. 5:11)

People sometimes come up to me and tell me some wonderful story of how in the past God has used me to bless them. They are often embarrassed about telling me, and usually start by saying "You must hear this all the time but ... " The truth is, like everyone else, I too need to hear encouraging words. I am too old to get bigheaded about what they say, I am just so thrilled that God has used me. We need to regularly build each other up by encouraging words.

Lord, help us to always encourage people.

Who do I know who at this time needs an extra portion of encouragement?

THURS

He lifted me out of the slimy pit, out of the mud and mire. (Psa. 40:2)

When I was a cowman, I would be up long before the crack of dawn, wading through deep mud and muck to collect my cows for milking. Sometimes my boots would get stuck in the deep mud and it was really hard to lift them out. Before I was a Christian things were not good and it was like being stuck in deep muck. Then I met Jesus, and since becoming a Christian, it's as though Jesus has lifted me out of that mess and put my feet on solid rock, which of course is much more pleasant to walk on, and a much better way to live.

“” **Lord, thank You for lifting us out of the mud and muck.**

? **Do I remember ever seeing anything stuck in mud?**

FRI

But you were washed ... (1 Cor. 6:11)

Yesterday I told you how when I was a cowman I would often get my boots very dirty. However, when you work with animals, it's not only your boots that get dirty and smelly. I also worked with pigs. Now some say that pigs are very clean animals but they do seem to love not only getting themselves messy, but also anyone who is working with them. It was wonderful at the end of the day to lie in a bath and have a good wash. The Bible tells us that the wrong things we do make us messy but that Jesus died on the cross to take away all that mess and to wash us clean again.

“” **Thank You, Lord, for making us clean inside.**

? **Which animals like to be clean and which animals like to be messy?**

SAT

They are shepherds who lack understanding; they all turn to their own way. (Isa. 56:11)

After the cows and the pigs, I must mention sheep. These seem to be the animals with the smallest brains, as all they do is eat grass and play Follow My Leader. When I had to look after them, I had to watch them the whole time – especially the pregnant ewes and the lambs – to make sure that they came to no harm. Isaiah was very annoyed with the shepherds who were supposed to be looking after the people of Israel because they were only looking after themselves. Let's always be looking for any around us that may need our help.

Lord, help us always to be willing to help others.

What farm animal would I most like to own?

Week 48

SUN

CD 2: 22

Away from me, you evildoers, that I may keep the commands of my God! (Psa. 119:115)

As Christians we will always be tempted to do wrong things by some of those around us. At one time or another, most young drivers have been encouraged by their passengers to drive their cars faster than is legal or safe and some sadly have not lived to tell the tale. We cannot blame others when we do wrong things, we have to be strong enough to say no, especially if people are trying to encourage us to do things which go against the teachings of God.

Lord, help us to be strong enough to say no when tempted to do wrong things.

What wrong things do I find it hardest to say no to?

MON

"No-one can serve two masters ... You cannot serve both God and Money." (Matt. 6:24)

Throughout a normal day I wonder if we spend as much time thinking and talking about God as we do thinking and talking about money. I have been in some church meetings where the introduction to the offering has been as long as the Bible talk. Our verse tells us that money is not just a coin or a note, it can be a master that we live for and serve. Christians beware, if we are thinking too much about money, we cannot be living for God as well.

Lord, help us to live for You and not for money.

How much of my day involves thinking about, talking about or spending money?

TUES

How great is the love the Father has lavished on us, that we should be called children of God! (1 John 3:1)

At one time it was just the Jewish nation who were known as the children of God, but since Jesus died and rose again all Christian believers, whatever their nationality, are known as God's children. Racism is a terrible thing where people are persecuted for the colour of their skin or for the country they come from. Christians should never be racist. As we all share the same Heavenly Father, we must all be brothers and sisters belonging to the same family whatever our skin colour.

Lord, please stop people being racist.

Why is it wrong to make fun of people from other countries?

WEDS

"Away with the noise of your songs! I will not listen to the music of your harps." (Amos 5:23)

I wonder how much of our meetings is taken up by music. For some maybe a quarter or maybe half, and for others most of the time together. Singing songs and playing musical instruments do nothing for God unless the people who are singing and playing are righteous and living for justice. Praising God is not about words being sung, but about the kind of life being lived and how people are being treated. It's sometimes good to have meetings without any music to give us time to focus on where we really are at with God.

Lord, help us to realise that it's more important to live *for You* than to sing *to You*.

What other ways are there of praising God in our meetings than with music?

THURS

Jesus did many other things as well. (John 21:25)

Then follows, *"If every one of them were written down, I suppose that even the whole world would not have room for the books that would be written."* This is incredible. We have got just four books in the Bible telling us about the life of Jesus, but those pages only contain a tiny fragment of the things that He did in His 33 years on earth. Imagine the conversations He had, the healings He did, the miracles He performed, that we know nothing about. Imagine what those disciples must have witnessed in three short years. Wow.

Lord, thank You that we can read the four Gospels which tell us a tiny bit about You.

What other wonderful things can I imagine Jesus did that are not written down in the Gospels?

FRI "If your enemy is hungry, give him food to eat." (Prov. 25:21)

Remember this was written in the time when revenge was OK with God. An eye for an eye and a tooth for a tooth was the Old Testament way of doing things. But this little proverb reflects a bit of the New Testament. Instead of retaliation: be wise, show kindness and it will be like heaping burning hot coals on the other person's head. This will make the person who has done wrong feel guilty and want to put things right. A punch on the nose heals quickly but living in guilt will not go away until it has been dealt with.

Lord, help us to show kindness to those who do wrong to us.

Can you see any differences between this proverb and what Jesus taught on how we should treat our enemies?

SAT All of them were filled with the Holy Spirit and began to speak in other tongues ... (Acts 2:4)

When I was filled with the Holy Spirit I really wanted to speak in other tongues but people kept telling me that tongues were not important. I didn't believe them. One night I walked up and down the beach in the rain and told God that I would not go to bed until He gave me this gift. And of course He did. Ever since then I have enjoyed praising God with those special words. Speaking in tongues is a gift from God, and all His gifts are important and available for Christians of all ages.

Lord, thank You that we are able to praise You in other tongues.

Are there times when I shouldn't speak in tongues?

SUN

CD 2: 23

... where the Spirit of the Lord is, there is freedom. (2 Cor. 3:17)

I have always loved the freedom of being outdoors, either running around a field or walking by the seaside. Before I was a Christian I remember spending just a few hours in a tiny prison cell for driving my car very dangerously. It was horrible being trapped in a small room with no window and the door locked. The Bible tells us that before we became Christians we were like prisoners but that Jesus died to set us free. With His Holy Spirit living inside us we can know real freedom. We must always remember that because Jesus died to set us free, we must never allow any person to put chains back on us again.

Lord, thank You for giving us freedom.

What would I miss the most if I was locked up in a prison?

MON

When his parents saw him, they were astonished. (Luke 2:48)

Jesus had gone missing and Mary and Joseph were frantically trying to find Him. Eventually when they did our verse says they were astonished. I wonder why. Was it because Jesus did not tell them where He was going, or was it because they found Him sitting with the highest level of religious leaders of the day asking them questions and listening to their answers? We may never know, but it is important to notice that Jesus was not teaching the religious leaders, He, like everyone else in the world needed to learn from others before He began to teach.

Lord, help us always to be willing to learn from others.

Do I find it hard to take teaching and advice from others?

TUES

Direct me in the path of your commands, for there I find delight.

(Psa. 119:35)

When I am staying away from home, I sometimes feel like going out for an Indian meal. Being in a strange place, I have been known to wander around for hours trying to find a restaurant and then when I have eventually found one, the meal is sometimes awful. Nowadays I always ask local people to direct me to a good restaurant and that way I save a lot of time and nearly always get a delicious meal. Life is full of choices and different paths to take, let's always ask God to direct us in the way we should go, then we too will end up at the best and right place.

Lord, please help us to listen to the directions that You give us.

If I have to ask for directions, would I ask anyone or just a certain type of person?

WEDS

A time to weep and a time to laugh. (Eccl. 3:4)

Once at one of my cell group meetings we spent time meditating on God, with a great big candle in the middle of the floor. Later in the evening one of our group was holding the candle and, feeling very sad, suddenly burst into tears. It was at this point the tears instantly extinguished the flame. It looked quite funny and I felt like laughing, but I knew I shouldn't. Fortunately for me in a very short time, my friend who was crying saw the funny side of things as well, so we all burst out laughing together. There is a right time to weep and a right time to laugh.

Lord, help us to know the right times to weep and the right times to laugh.

Have I ever been in a situation when I have wanted to laugh but have had to hold back my laughter?

THURS A time to mourn and a time to dance. (Eccl. 3:4)

Soon after the tragic bombing of the twin towers in New York, I was invited to lead a family service in the West of England. I asked the organisers if it would be appropriate, as we were all in a time of shock and mourning and my family services include a time of praise and dancing. After discussion, we decided to carry on and have the meeting, and it was a great time. Although we could never forget all those who had died or lost loved ones, we also felt that it was important to praise God. Mourning and dance do not always go together, but mourning and worshipping God do.

Lord, even in times of mourning, we pray that we will never stop praising You.

What do I think of people dancing in church meetings.

FRI "Consider carefully what you hear." (Mark 4:24)

It's very easy to listen to someone and get completely the wrong message. I wonder how many times we have said to people, "Oh I'm sorry I thought you meant ..." but that was not what they had meant at all. Jesus kept saying, "If anyone has ears to hear, let him hear", in other words, as our verse says, consider carefully what you are listening to. When we listen to family, friends or even preachers, let's listen carefully because often we react and get hurt unnecessarily, just because we did not really hear what the person said.

Lord, help us to really listen to what is being said.

When did I last listen to someone and get the wrong message?

SAT The Lord has taken away your punishment ... (Zeph. 3:15)

When I was about eleven years old I spent a short time at a boarding school. On one of my first nights away from home someone threw a stone through our dormitory window and all the boys in the room ran into the corridor to see what had happened. It was then one of the masters saw us and punished us all by giving us the cane for getting out of our beds. Rather unfair punishment, I thought at the time. Although we all deserve to be punished for the sinful lives we have led, the perfect Jesus was punished in our place by dying for us on a cross. We should be so grateful.

Thank You, Lord, for taking our punishment for us.

What are the best and worst types of punishment?

Week 50

SUN And after the fire came a gentle whisper. (1 Kings 19:12)

CD 2: 24

I love hearing a storm raging outside, especially if I am sitting by a nice warm fire. I feel safe knowing that the elements outside cannot affect me. Elijah was in a cave when he saw the power of a mighty wind, felt an earthquake and then the heat from the fire around him. God is powerful and often when we see the awesome power of the weather and the elements, it reminds us of this. But God was not in the wind, earthquake and fire. His power was found in a gentle whisper. Almighty God, the Creator of the universe has not come to shout at us or frighten us with His power, rather, He loves to gently whisper in our ears His plans for us, like a dad speaking to a small child.

Lord, help us to always be listening when You whisper Your messages to us.

How does God speak to us today?

MON

"But when you pray, go into your room, close the door and pray to your Father." (Matt. 6:6)

In Bible times some people enjoyed making a great performance out of praying to impress those around them and to make their audience think that they were very spiritual. Today in our meetings we can still try and impress people with our prayers or by making an exhibition of ourselves while pretending to praise. It's good to pray with others, but it's even more important to spend time praying to Father by ourselves in the quiet of our own rooms.

Lord, we just want to impress You, not those around us.

In what ways is it possible to "show off" in church meetings?

TUES

"There are six days for work. So come and be healed on those days, not on the Sabbath." (Luke 13:14)

The Pharisees loved making up Sabbath laws. They decreed that you were not allowed to tie a knot in a rope, but you were allowed to tie a woman's belt. So to get water from a well on the Sabbath you had to use a woman's belt! They also stated that nothing could be carried by a hand, chest or shoulder, but you could carry things with the *back* of your hand, your foot, mouth, elbow, ear, hair or shoe. They even tried to ban healing and that is when Jesus became very annoyed with them and called them hypocrites. The Pharisees hated Jesus but the people loved what He was doing.

Lord, it's wonderful to live under grace and not all those laws.

Is it right to have rules for Sundays especially as the Sabbath is on a Saturday?

WEDS The Lord is my shepherd, I shall not be in want. (Psa. 23:1)

Often I really want something. Then I think I really *need* it and am sure that I will not be really happy until I get it. Maybe if I pray about it the Lord will give me the money to go out and buy it. So often the things we think we need are just things that we want, and some of these things we don't get because the Lord knows that we would be better off without them. The Good Shepherd looks after both the sheep and the lambs and, while He will always provide our needs, He will not always provide our wants.

Lord, we know You don't provide all our "wants", but thank You for providing all our needs.

What do I need at this moment?

THURS Do not eat the food of a stingy man ... (Prov. 23:6)

This is followed in verse 7 by *"for he is the kind of man who is always thinking about the cost"*. It's sad that quite a few Christians are stingy. They are always looking for discounts, negotiating bargains and whenever you go out for a meal with them they complain about the prices. These people are not a lot of fun to be with, and end up with very few real friends. Let's be generous. Let's leave good tips if the food and service is good, let's always be willing to buy the first round of drinks, and let's show people that because God is generous to us we are always going to be generous to others.

Lord, help us never to be stingy.

How do people see me, generous or a bit mean?

FRI

So they hurried off and found Mary and Joseph, and the baby, who was lying in a manger. (Luke 2:16)

The shepherds were simple guys who lived for their sheep but as soon as the angel appeared and told them about the birth of Jesus, they left everything to run and find Him. I suppose they must have thought the stable was a strange place to find the Saviour, but they were scared stiff of the angel and hardly likely to argue the fact. I think it's wonderful that the ordinary shepherds were the first people to worship Jesus; the clever wise men did not arrive till much later.

Lord, thank You for loving ordinary people and not just the very clever people.

Do you think that the shepherds' lives changed once they had seen Jesus?

SAT

He who has the Son has life; he who does not have the Son of God does not have life. (1 John 5:12)

It's hard to imagine but all around us are living people who have yet to start living. They laugh, cry, walk and run, sleep and wake, but according to the Bible they are not really alive. When we gave our lives to the Lord Jesus, He gave His life to us and that meant that He breathed real life into every part of our being. There is no one on earth that can enjoy living as much as a Christian can. I hope those around us who are not yet Christians can see how much we appreciate being alive.

Lord, thank You for making our lives so good.

What differences can people see between me, and those who are not yet Christians?

SUN

CD 2: 25

"Heaven and earth will pass away, but my words will never pass away." (Matt. 24:35)

When I first buy a car it looks brand new, even if it is not. It has been polished so that I can see my face in it, the chrome sparkles in the sun and even the tyres have not one bit of mud or dirt on them. It looks as though it will last me a lifetime. After a few months, however, you would not recognise it as the same car, not because I have neglected to look after it, but because I have driven it many thousands of miles and it has depreciated rapidly. As I look at it, I know it will not last more than a few years tops. As we look around us at the earth or stare up into the vast heavens, these too, like my poor old car, were not made to last forever. However, the words that Jesus spoke will last forever and will never pass away.

Thank You, Lord, that Your words will last forever.

Have I ever bought anything that didn't last long?

MON

All kinds of animals, birds, reptiles and creatures of the sea are being tamed ... (James 3:7)

If I switch on my TV I can watch programmes about wild animals or I can watch programmes about family pets. I always prefer to watch the wild animals, as they seem so much more exciting. Keeping pets may be exciting but watching them I think is boring. There are many programmes now of wild animals that have been tamed and have become family pets, and I find these just as boring. The Bible tells us that although most creatures can be tamed the little pink thing inside our mouths cannot be. Our tongue and the words we say can hurt people much more than any wild animal can.

Lord, please help us to think before we speak.

What pet would I most like to have?

TUES "Son of man, can these bones live?" (Ezek. 37:3)

Ezekiel was in a valley surrounded by dry bones and God asked him the question, "Can these bones live?" Although Ezekiel answered "Sovereign Lord, you alone know", we would have probably answered no. These bones were once living people who must have died years before and no one could put life back into old bones, could they? Well, no one except God that is. God put flesh on the bones, then breathed life into the bodies and they stood up and became a vast army. It's easy for us as Christians to become dry and seem to have little of the exciting life of Jesus in us. Every day we need to ask Jesus to breath fresh life into us so we stay full of His Holy Spirit and able to do all He asks us to.

" **Lord, please help us not to be dry and lifeless Christians.**

? **Have I ever been in a situation where I have not known the answer and thought, only God knows?**

WEDS An elder must be blameless, the husband of but one wife. (Titus 1:6)

In New Testament times an elder of a church had to fulfil many criteria and following this verse is a list of qualifications that he was expected to obey and observe. Notice I said *he* because an elder was always male in biblical times. Leading God's people is a very responsible position, and I think that we all should try and meet these qualifications if we oversee any group of people, including the youth and children. All of us would do well to read verses 5–9 and see if we match up to what was required of the biblical elder, not giving up if we don't, but certainly making every effort to try and do so.

" **Lord, help us to keep high standards in whatever work you call us to do.**

? **Are there areas that I could improve on as I read verses 5–9?**

THURS

"I am the Lord's servant," Mary answered. "May it be to me as you have said." (Luke 1:38)

Mary would have been a young teenager at the time the angel visited her and told her that she was going to become pregnant and give birth to a very special baby, the Son of God. Mary I'm sure would have had many questions, maybe even fears, but she trusted the angel and knew that whatever was going to happen, it was going to be what God wanted to happen. I wonder if there have been times when God has spoken to us but we have not done what He has wanted because either we have been afraid or thought it impossible. Let's learn from Mary and trust the Lord in everything.

Lord, help us, like Mary, to trust You, even in things we may not understand.

If I were a young teenage girl, how would I have reacted to the angel's message?

FRI

"My people are determined to turn from me." (Hos. 11:7)

There have been times in my life when I have deliberately sinned against God. There is something that I am determined to do that I know is wrong, Jesus even whispers to me "Don't do it", but I ignore Him. I want to do it and so I do it. A very short while later, I feel terrible. I have not just made a mistake, it's not an accident, I have no excuses. I am guilty of deliberately turning away from God and doing my own thing. The good news is that God still loves me and will forgive me if I say sorry, but I also know that He wants me to make every effort not to hurt Him and do that deliberate sin again.

Lord, please help us not to deliberately do wrong things.

Can I think of anything that I have done, that I knew was wrong, yet carried on and did it?

SAT Snatch others from the fire and save them. (Jude v.23)

Often we read in our newspapers about heroic firefighters. We read how they arrive at a house that is blazing and rush in, risking their lives to save the life of a child in an upstairs bedroom. We are told in Scripture that the future of those who are lost and do not give their lives to Jesus is a grim one. We are to be like the heroic firefighter and rush to save people from the fire by telling them about the love of Jesus, so that they too can believe in Him and then enjoy the wonderful life that only Jesus can give them, forever.

Lord, help us to see the urgency of telling people about You.

Let's talk about the good and bad points of being a firefighter.

Week 52

SUN "The Lord bless you and keep you ... make his face to shine upon you and be gracious to you ..." (Num. 6:24–25)

CD 2: 26

The next verse says *"the Lord turn his face towards you and give you peace"*. This was the priestly blessing that Aaron and his fellow priests were told by God to say over Israel. I love it when we end our meetings by blessing one another. I usually ask everyone to hold hands and say the words together, and I always tell them to keep their eyes open and look at each other as they say the words. It's easy to bless people with your eyes closed and you don't have to look at them, especially if there are people who we do not get on with. God wants us to mean what we are saying so, before we bless each other, we must put things right with the family of God.

Lord, as we bless people, help us to mean what we say.

If I had to bless people with my eyes open, are there people in my church that I would find it hard to look at?

MON

When God created man, he made him in the likeness of God. (Gen. 5:1)

Most of us are not really happy with the way that God made us. (Some of us would just like to be younger and fitter so we could play the sports that we used to enjoy.) Some of us would like to be taller or shorter or fatter or thinner, and nearly everyone would like to be better looking. God made us to look like we do because He not only wanted it that way, but because we are unique and there is no one else identical to us in the world – even identical twins are different. God loves us the way He made us, and He wants us to love ourselves the way He made us as well; after all, we are made in His image.

Lord, help us to love the "me" we see in the mirror.

How are my looks and personality different from those sitting with me now?

TUES

We must pay more careful attention ... to what we have heard, so that we do not drift away. (Heb. 2:1)

People tell me that I have a low attention level. That means I find it hard to concentrate on one subject for any length of time. At school the teacher always told me to pay attention, but after a short while my mind had drifted off and I was thinking about something else. I guess that is why I find it so easy to write fiction. As a Christian, though, I must pay attention to what others teach me and what the Bible says, otherwise I could easily drift away from the truth and end up just doing my own thing, and not what God wants me to do.

Lord, help us to pay attention to the people who teach us about You.

Do I find it easy to pay attention, or do I keep changing the subject as I talk with people?

WEDS

Precious in the sight of the Lord is the death of his saints. (Psa. 116:15)

Throughout the Roman Empire, many Christians died in terrible ways because they refused to deny Jesus and obey the evil Caesars. If we read our history books we will also discover that from then until now brave Christians have been killed, their only crime being that they were followers of Jesus. Even today in some countries in the world Christians are still being persecuted and martyred. But everyone who dies for the Lord is very precious to Him and does not go unnoticed. The Bible even says that they will get a special crown in heaven. Let's never forget that many Christians gave their lives so that we could have our own Bibles and enjoy the freedom to worship that we have today.

Lord, thank You for the freedom we have to worship You.

How many people can I think of who have died because of their faith in Christ?

THURS

Philip found Nathanael and told him ... (John 1:44)

Jesus said to Philip, "Follow me." The next thing we read is that Philip is so excited about meeting Jesus that he ran off straightaway to find his friend Nathanael, and when he found him he told him that they had found the one whom Moses and the prophets wrote about, Jesus of Nazareth. I wonder if we are still that excited about Jesus. We have friends all around us who do not yet know Him, I wonder if we, like Philip, can't wait to have the opportunity to tell them about Him. If we really love Jesus and believe He is the Saviour of the world, I think we should feel this way, don't you?

Lord, help us to be like Philip and want to share the good news of Jesus with others.

When was the last time I talked about Jesus to someone who is not yet a Christian?

FRI

So Joshua burned Ai and made it a permanent heap of ruins ...

(Josh. 8:28)

God was not pleased with the city of Ai, so after Joshua had conquered it, he burnt it to the ground. I remember that before I was a Christian I had a very large collection of records. Some of these were OK, but many of these were not very good albums for a Christian to own, plus as I listened to them they would bring bad memories into my mind. So when I became a Christian I asked my Dad to burn them all. They would be no help to me as I began my walk with Jesus, and they would forever be a reminder of the bad old days.

Lord, please show us if we have things which You are not happy with us possessing.

Do I own anything that may be unhelpful and reminds me of the "bad old days"?

SAT

"Go and make a careful search for the child ... so that I too may go and worship him." (Matt. 2:8)

Herod was a wicked, evil king and insanely jealous of anyone who might take his throne away from him. The wise men came to ask for directions but once they had found Jesus, they did not go back and tell Herod where He was. It took the wise men many years to find Jesus. Perhaps we have relatives who are still searching for truth, yet have still not yet found Jesus. Some people spend longer than others on their journey, let's keep praying for them because if they really are seeking, in time they will find.

Lord, help us never to try and rush someone into becoming a follower of Yours.

Remind each other of all that happened when Jesus was born 2,000 years ago.

GOOD FRIDAY

Jesus said, "It is finished." With that, he bowed his head and gave up his spirit.

(John 19:30)

The last cry from Jesus on the cross was not a cry of defeat, it was the great victory shout. His mission while on earth was to defeat Satan and provide a way for boys, girls, men and women to be made right with Father God. By the age of thirty-three Jesus had completed His task and so it was now time to return back home to His Father. On this special day, we do feel very sad as we remember the terrible way that Jesus suffered, but it's not all sadness, because our Bibles tell us that we do not have to wait until Easter Sunday before we can be joyful. "Good Friday" should be renamed "the very best Friday", as this is the day when we celebrate Jesus shouting "Mission accomplished!"

Lord, because You suffered terrible pain, we now know that all the wrong things that we have done have been forgiven. Thank You.

What would Jesus like me to do today to really celebrate the "best Friday"?

EASTER SUNDAY

The angel said to the women, "Do not be afraid ... He is not here; he has risen ..."

(Matt. 28:5–6)

The two Marys arrived at the tomb very sad because their best friend Jesus was dead, then suddenly they met the angel. Now the angel had already shown himself to the guards who, we are told, were so scared they shook and then passed out. Now when the angel appeared to the two Marys, understandably, they too were frightened at first, but once they heard the news that Jesus was alive, their fear turned to great joy and they ran to tell the rest of Jesus' friends the great news. Let's remember on this wonderful Easter Day that although Jesus had to die so all our wrong doings could be forgiven, He also came back to life again. Let us, like the Marys, be full of joy today, and not be frightened to tell all our friends that Jesus is alive.

Lord, it's great to know that You are alive today.

What do I think that the risen Jesus is doing now, at this very minute?

CHRISTMAS DAY

The time came for the baby to be born, and she gave birth to her firstborn, a son.

(Luke 2:6–7)

Although December 25th is probably nowhere near the actual date that the Lord Jesus was born, millions of people throughout the world hold this day special and remember the wonderful, miraculous birth of the King of kings. No palace but an animal dwelling, no soft bed or clean sheets but straw and a feeding trough, and no medical help or nurses just Joseph and maybe one or two people who were nearby. But out of this poor stable came God's Son, who would change the world – forever. We may not be rich, some of us were born in poor areas, but rich or poor does not matter, Jesus wants all of us to live for Him and by doing this, we too can help change the world.

Lord, help us to give thanks for Your birth not just on December 25th, but all year round.

Can I think of any people who started life very poor, but were greatly used by God?